Cookout USA

Grilling Favorites
Coast to Coast

by **GEORGIA ORCUTT**
and **JOHN MARGOLIES**

CHRONICLE BOOKS
SAN FRANCISCO

Library of Congress Cataloging-in-Publication Data available.

ISBN 0-8118-4738-1

Manufactured in China.

Designed by Margo Mooney

Distributed in Canada by Raincoast Books
9050 Shaughnessy Street
Vancouver, British Columbia V6P 6E5

10 9 8 7 6 5 4 3 2 1

Chronicle Books LLC
85 Second Street
San Francisco, California 94105

www.chroniclebooks.com

DEDICATION

To Stephen, Eli, and Amos, who tasted everything and never had to wonder what was for dinner.

—Georgia Orcutt

ACKNOWLEDGMENTS

We'd like to thank the following people for their generous help in making this book happen: Margo Mooney, for her energy, enthusiasm, and talent; Amy Treadwell and Ayako Akazawa at Chronicle Books, for believing in this idea and watching over it at every stage of production; our agents, Jim Fitzgerald and Wendy Burton Brouws, for their support and encouragement; Lew and Janet Baer, Jim Heimann, Leland and Crystal Payton, Don and Newly Preziosi, and Sharon Wolf, for making images available to us from their ephemera collections; and Susan Kendall, Kevin Daley, Jane Doerfer, Cynthia VanHazinga, Margie Hilton, Gilly Puttick, and John Glyphis, for contributing opinions on recipes.

CHARCOALMANSHIP

cooking on the outside, smiling on the inside

ANY AMATEUR CHEF worthy of his salt and other spices should be aware of the advantages inherent in outdoor barbecuing. A situation is created in which the male assumes complete control, while delighted damsels sit admiringly on the sidelines. The elemental environment of nature, in which cocktails combine with the atmosphere to enhance appetite, builds maximum anticipation for eating a memorable meal. And, most important of all,

food

BY THOMAS MARIO

Contents

Leave it to Henry Ford to set us on the right road. In the early 1920s, he foresaw the culinary future of charcoal, and collaborated with his friend Thomas Edison to open America's first charcoal briquette plant. In the decades since, the United States has become the cookout nation. We're crazy about grilling and dining alfresco, whether it's the Fourth of July or any old day.

From California to Maine, from Minnesota to Alabama, we love to cook meat, seafood, poultry, vegetables, and fruits outdoors and to find clever ways to experiment by soaking them in marinades, slathering them with spice rubs, mopping them with sops, and brushing them with sauces. We delight in all the fixings, too, especially those that simply shout summer: potato salad, baked beans, coleslaw, and watermelon.

We're fiercely proud of our favorite methods, mixtures, and definitions. In the Northeast, we might invite friends over for "a barbecue" and cook a few steaks on the grill; in much of the country, we eat "barbecue," referring to meat slowly roasted in a smoker and enhanced with spices and sauce. Barbecue joints offering takeout do the cooking for many of us. In fact, cookouts have become a spectator sport on the barbecue cook-off circuit, which includes two extravaganzas with hundreds of cooks and thousands of visitors: Memphis in May ("The Super Bowl of Swine"), and American Royal, held in Kansas City in October. Both cities claim to be the Barbecue Capital of the U.S.A.

The sun is shining, friends and family are all around, and it's time to get the party going, in your backyard or at the beach. So come along with us on a cookout journey through all of the fifty states. Our grand tour offers you a chance to sample a wide range of cooking styles, regional flavors, and fancies.

If you choose, you can shop online to find honest-to-goodness local ingredients, from Hawaiian-grown pineapples to

Wisconsin-crafted bratwurst, but you don't need to go farther than your neighborhood supermarket to buy what you need for great cookouts. Every recipe you discover on this trip can be prepared using a backyard charcoal or gas grill, and all the marinades and sauces can be made with pantry basics. So, let's get started.

If you like beef, stop in Kentucky for sirloin steak marinated in bourbon, detour to Nevada for a juicy prime rib, or travel across Texas for a tasty brisket. If you prefer fish, head to Alaska for spicy halibut, or come to Florida for saucy grouper. If you avoid eating meat, travel to California for grilled vegetables, continue on to Illinois for roasted corn on the cob, or go to Georgia for memorable and oh-so-sweet Vidalia onions.

Try some new ways of grilling, too. In Arizona, flavor your fowl with mesquite; in Massachusetts, take some time to smoke a whole turkey; in Washington, plunk your salmon on a wooden plank; in Utah, do up a cherry cobbler in a Dutch oven. Take a walk on the wild side, if you wish: in Delaware, grill duck; in Maine, make it lobster; in Maryland, try soft-shell crabs; in New Hampshire, sample some venison; and in Wyoming, why not elk?

So many choices—and yes, it's hard to stay in just one place. But you don't have to, ever again. Today, you can buy a folding grill that fits easily into the trunk of your car. Henry Ford would be so happy.

If you're in the market for a new grill, go online and visit your local retailers to see the staggering number of choices. The four main categories—charcoal, gas, electric, and smoker—come in many shapes and sizes, with a range of prices to match. You can buy a small cast-iron hibachi charcoal grill for under $25, or go all out and spend $10,000 on a stainless-steel gas grill. You can choose a grill shaped like a cow or a pig that also burns wood pellets, or settle on a steel grill with cast-iron cooking grates and rosewood prep shelves. And, there are hundreds of gadgets to make grilling easier: mitts that defy heat, long-handled tongs, spatulas for fish, nonstick rib racks, mesh grill baskets to keep small foods from slipping into the fire, thermometers to measure grill heat or instantly read the interior temperature of what you're cooking, and all sorts of skewers.

But no matter how many bells and whistles your grill contains, its main job is to cook your food and deliver great flavor. To help you in your backyard odyssey this cookout season, we offer these words of advice.

● When you cook, keep your grill a good 10 feet from any building. And never, ever use your grill indoors. Each year in the United States there are a number of deaths from carbon monoxide poisoning resulting from indoor grilling.

Barbecuing

Selection of Steaks

The meat man is a barbecue chef's best friend. So let him know that your purchase is to be barbecued. Select fine-quality beef that is well marbled with fat. For a large crowd, a sirloin steak is your best choice. It is the easiest to slice for sandwiches and wonderful for just plain eating! Other

12

● Use a glass or ceramic dish, or a heavy-duty zip-top plastic bag for marinating meats or poultry. Avoid cast-iron or aluminum containers, which can react with acidic ingredients. If the food isn't covered with the marinade, turn it several times, or flip the plastic bag over, to provide an even coating.

● Discard leftover marinades that have come in contact with raw food to destroy bacteria that may have formed. If you want to use the marinade as a basting sauce, be sure to cook the food for at least 5 minutes after you brush it on; otherwise, bring the marinade to a boil first. Or, use reserved marinade that hasn't come in contact with raw food. And always put cooked food on clean platters, not the same ones used for raw food.

● Keep the cooking grate as clean as you would a skillet in the kitchen to prevent food from sticking. Scrub it with a wire grill brush or steel wool after your meal, and brush it with oil just before you start cooking again.

● Use long-handled tongs, not a fork, to turn food. Every time you stab a piece of chicken or a steak, you create a place for juice to run out. And try not to flip-flop. With just a few exceptions, such as foods that cook quickly or tend to burn, turn food just once during the grilling process for even cooking and to seal in the juices.

● To avoid flare-ups, use lean cuts of meat or trim off excess fat. Drain off excess marinade before putting food on the grill.

● Experiment with wood chips and wood chunks to coax extra flavor from all grilled foods. You can find hickory, oak, maple, cherry, apple, mesquite, and a range of other woods for sale online, at upscale grocery stores, and at stores that sell grills. Chips are thin shavings that burn quickly, and are best used for quick-cooking foods; chunks range from golf-ball size to baseball size, burn more slowly, and are best for long-cooking foods. As a general rule, soak chips and chunks for at least 1 hour before adding them to the fire. (Read the manufacturer's directions before adding wood chips or chunks to a gas grill; some models come with a smoker box for this purpose, or will recommend using a diffuser

pan. If you add soaked chips directly to lava rocks, they can burn too fast.) To slow down the burning time of smoking woods, for both charcoal and gas grills, try this trick: Lay out a piece of heavy-duty aluminum foil about 2½ feet long and arrange several handfuls of chips or chunks in the center. Bring the foil up on both sides and crimp it around the edges to form a tight packet. Poke 4 random holes in the packet with a chop-stick. Place the packet on top of hot coals or heated lava rocks.

For Gas Grills

● Don't use a propane cylinder that is dented, corroded, or rusty.

● If you aren't sure how much propane is left in your cylinder, run a wet finger down the side, or dip a paintbrush in water and paint a single stripe from top to bottom. The wet streak evaporates faster over the empty part of the cylinder.

● Before lighting the grill, make sure the cylinder is properly attached. Always open the lid before lighting.

For Charcoal Grills

● Use a round stainless-steel cylinder called a charcoal chimney, rather than petroleum-based lighter fluid, to start the fire. Simply place the chimney on the grill, put several crumpled-up newspapers in the bottom, and fill about halfway with charcoal. Light through the openings in the sides. In about 15 minutes, when the charcoal is burning, lift up the chimney and let the hot coals spill out onto the bottom of the grill. Add more coals as necessary.

● Several companies now sell natural hardwood charcoal, which reaches cooking temperatures sooner than briquettes and contains no fillers or chemicals. Read the instructions on the bag.

● For food that requires several hours to cook, once the fire gets going you'll need to add more charcoal every 30 to 45 minutes to maintain even heat.

● Putting the food on the grill too soon—when the coals are too hot—is one of the major causes of cookout disasters. Wait until there are no flames, and the coals are a whitish gray around the edges.

Determining Grill Temperature

Cookout cooking isn't an exact science, which is part of its charm. Personal taste also comes into play. Remember the kids who loved to eat blackened marshmallows while you were carefully browning yours? Whatever you prefer, it's helpful to have a good estimate of your grill's temperature.

Gas grills come with temperature gauges that eliminate the guesswork. To judge the heat of a charcoal fire, try this trick: Very carefully hold your hand, palm side down, 4 to 6 inches above the coals and count the number of seconds you can keep it there. The temperature is low (about 325°F) if you can count to 5 seconds; medium (350°F) is 4 seconds, medium-hot (375°F) is 3 seconds, and hot (400°F to 425°F) is 1 to 2 seconds.

The proximity of coals to one another affects the grill temperature. If you want a hotter fire, add more coals and keep them close together or in several layers. If you want to reduce the heat, spread the coals farther apart.

HERE IS **Your FREE GIFT** (SEE OTHER SIDE)

Guaranteed by Good Housekeeping REPLACEMENT OR A REFUND OF MONEY IF NOT AS ADVERTISED THEREIN

Adjustable "SAF-T-GRILL"

LARGE 13½" BOWL

Rubber-Tipped Detachable Legs

Nationally Advertised! Portable, Steel
BAR-B-CUE Charcoal BRAZIER

Indirect Heat

When placed over a bed of hot coals, foods such as burgers, hot dogs, steaks, fish, and vegetables cook in a matter of minutes. But to accommodate slower-cooking foods such as roasts, whole chickens, or a rack of ribs, your grill should be set up for indirect cooking, making it more of an oven than a broiler. There are two ways to arrange the coals to make this happen:

1. Build a hot fire using several layers of coals, and when they are ready for cooking, use a hand-held hoe or small shovel to mound them over onto one side of the grill. Put a drip pan on the other side of the fuel bed. Place the food on the grill over the drip pan, and turn the food several times for even cooking. (In a gas grill, preheat the grill using all the burners, then turn off one burner and place the food above it.)

2. Build a hot fire as above and arrange the coals in a ring around the outside edges of the fuel bed, about 4 inches high and about 5 inches across. This allows a space in the center to position a pan to catch drippings or hold liquid and moisten the food as it cooks. (You can buy drip pans in your local hardware store, or use disposable heavy-duty aluminum baking pans from the grocery store.) The ring method works well for cooking whole turkeys, which won't fit on half of the grill, but it takes more vigilance to add more coals and keep the fire burning evenly.

During the cooking process you'll need to add more charcoal to keep the fire burning evenly, every 30 minutes or so if you're using hard-wood charcoal and about every 45 minutes or so if you're using briquettes. A hinged grate is ideal for this purpose. If you don't have one, you will have to lift off the entire grate and whatever is on it when you need to add charcoal. To make this easier, stand two bricks or cinder blocks on end lengthwise about 10 inches apart on the ground near your grill. Wearing oven mitts, carefully lift off the grate and position it on the bricks or blocks. Add another layer of charcoal, reposition the grate, and cover the grill as quickly as possible. And try not to peek. Every time you take the lid off the grill, you lose heat and slow down the cooking process.

ARKANSAS
LOUISIANA
ALABAMA
Jackson

234
4:28
251
4:55
Montgomery
208

292
5:24
354
6:41
275

Greetings from ALABAMA   TROY

Chicken Breasts with White Barbecue Sauce

In some parts of Alabama, especially the northern sections, barbecue sauce is white, not red as it is in most of the country. Since 1925, white sauce has been a signature condiment at Big Bob Gibson's in Decatur, and the restaurant's special blend, which is sold online, won first place in Kansas City's American Royal Barbecue Contest in 1995. It can be used as a marinade or as a table sauce for chicken and pork. Several companies sell their own special versions on the Web. You can make up a batch before your cookout to serve with just about anything, but since it contains mayonnaise, keep it refrigerated until you're ready to serve it. Here, it's paired with chicken, another food closely associated with the Cotton State. Alabama ranks third in the nation in the production of broiler chickens—some 1.1 billion annually. Serve this tasty chicken with a green salad.

4   boneless, skinless chicken breast halves (about 8 ounces each)

ALABAMA WHITE SAUCE

½   cup mayonnaise

½   cup cider vinegar

1   tablespoon fresh lemon juice

½   teaspoon cayenne pepper, or more to taste

Salt and freshly ground black pepper to taste

The night before grilling, place the chicken breasts in a glass dish to marinate.

To make the Alabama white sauce: Combine all the ingredients in a medium non-reactive bowl and whisk until smooth. Pour half the sauce over the chicken, turn each piece to coat well, cover with plastic wrap, and refrigerate overnight. Cover and refrigerate the reserved sauce.

Build a medium fire in a charcoal grill or heat a gas grill to 350°F. Remove the chicken from the marinade and place on paper towels, turning each piece to remove any marinade that clings

COOK-OUT RECIPES

compliments of

ROYAL HOST COFFEE

to the meat. Spoon ¼ cup of the reserved sauce into a small bowl to use just for basting. Oil the grill grate well and brush the tops of the chicken with some of the reserved basting sauce. Cook for 3 minutes, turn, and brush the tops again with the reserved basting sauce. Cook for 3 minutes longer, or until the chicken is fork-tender. Watch carefully to be sure it doesn't burn. Transfer to a platter. Serve with the remaining reserved white sauce for dipping.

Serves 4

Spicy Grilled Chili-Lime Halibut

The largest halibut ever caught by a sportfisherman in the United States weighed 459 pounds and came from the waters of Unalaska Bay. Although that fish was a candidate for the record books, popular charter boat excursions to halibut fishing grounds in Kachemak Bay, Cook Inlet, and the Gulf of Alaska usually hope to catch one weighing around 200 pounds. Halibut is serious business in Alaska, where commercial fishing operations bring in about 25,000 tons annually. With its clean, sweet flavor and firm, flaky meat, halibut is a good fish for grilling. When cooking this fish, or any other, be sure the grill is scrupulously clean and lightly oiled, to prevent sticking. Serve with Crispy Idaho Potato Wedges (page 34). If you can't find halibut, use cod, haddock, salmon, or shark.

4	halibut steaks (4 to 6 ounces each), preferably ½ inch thick
½	cup rice vinegar
½	cup fresh lime juice
¼	cup grapeseed oil or olive oil
1	cup Thai chili sauce
¼	cup black sesame seeds

One to 2 hours before grilling, put the halibut steaks in a large nonreactive baking dish. Combine all the remaining ingredients in a small nonreactive bowl and stir with a whisk until blended. Pour the mixture over the fish, and turn the steaks so both sides are well covered with the marinade. Cover with plastic wrap and refrigerate for 1 to 2 hours, turning the steaks once. Remove the steaks from the refrigerator 30 minutes before cooking.

Build a medium fire in a charcoal grill or heat a gas grill to 350°F. Oil the grill grate. Place the steaks on the grate and cook for about 5 minutes on each side, carefully turning them with a metal spatula. The fish is done when it flakes easily when tested with a fork.

Serves 4

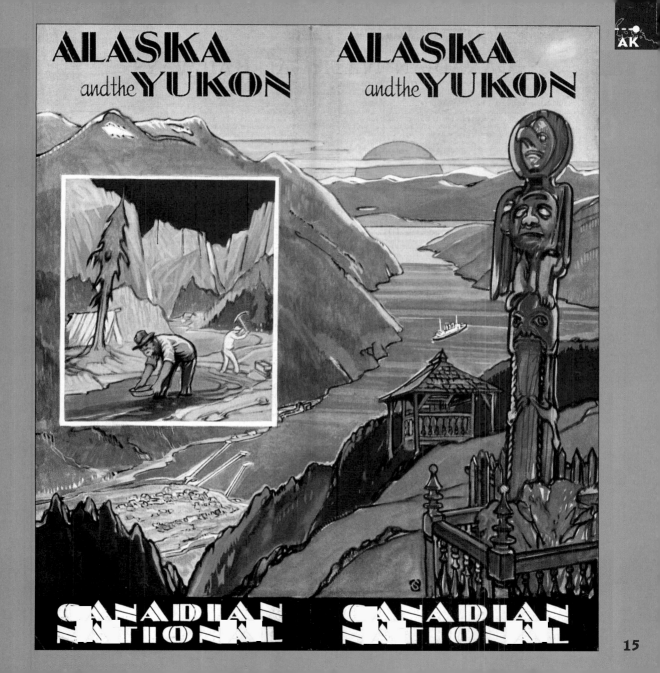

ALASKA and the YUKON

CANADIAN NATIONAL

15

ARIZONA

Phoenix 236
368
233
4:56
5:11
Springerville
ALBUQUERQUE
418
8:0

Mesquite-Grilled Chicken with Citrus-Ginger Sauce

small, thorny tree commonly found in the Southwest desert, the tenacious, quick-spreading mesquite is a curse when you're trying to eradicate it from open land, but a blessing for conservation efforts to prevent erosion. Mesquite wood in the form of chips, chunks, and charcoal is popular with outdoor cooks throughout the Southwest because it lends an earthy flavor to food. Use mesquite charcoal for this recipe. (You can find it online.) Serve with rice and an orange and avocado salad, if you like.

2 tablespoons olive oil

½ cup fresh orange juice

4 cloves garlic, minced

2 teaspoons minced fresh ginger

4 boneless, skinless chicken breast halves (about 8 ounces each)

CITRUS-GINGER SAUCE

1 tablespoon olive oil

3 scallions, white part only, minced

1 tablespoon minced fresh ginger (about a 2-inch piece)

½ cup lime juice

½ cup orange marmalade

¼ cup Cointreau or other orange-flavored liqueur

Salt and freshly ground black pepper to taste

The night before grilling, combine the olive oil, orange juice, garlic, and ginger in a large nonreactive baking dish and blend with a whisk. Add the chicken breasts, turn once, cover with plastic wrap, and refrigerate overnight.

Build a medium fire in a charcoal grill using mesquite charcoal. Oil the grill grate. Remove the chicken from the refrigerator.

To make the citrus-ginger sauce: Heat the olive oil in a medium nonreactive saucepan over low heat and sauté the scallions and ginger for 5 minutes, or until the onions are translucent and the ginger is soft. Add the lime juice, marmalade, and liqueur. Increase the heat to medium-hot and cook, stirring constantly, for several minutes, until the sauce is smooth and bubbling. Reduce the heat to low and simmer the sauce for 10 minutes, or until thickened and

MESA ARIZONA

IN ARIZONA'S VALLEY OF THE SUN IN ARIZONA'S VALLEY OF THE SUN

reduced by about a third. Season with salt and pepper. Remove the sauce and set aside. It will thicken further as it sits.

Remove the chicken from the marinade with tongs and place on the grate. Discard the marinade. Cook the chicken for 5 minutes on each side, or until fork-tender. Meanwhile, reheat the sauce. Serve the chicken with the sauce spooned on top.

Serves 4

17

Barbecued Pork Salad

During his White House days, Bill Clinton was such a fan of barbecued beef and pork ribs from McClard's Barbecue in Hot Springs, his boyhood home, that he had it catered aboard Air Force One. In the summer of 2004, in response to the former president's heart surgery, Scott McClard adjusted his menu to include sliced pork or beef served with beans and coleslaw, without bread or added sugar. A different take on barbecue, this salad is making its way onto menus throughout the state. Although much of the state's legendary barbecue is cooked slowly for hours in a smoker, this version works well on a backyard grill. The secret is in the sauce. This recipe makes about 8 cups of sauce, more than you will need here. Use the leftover sauce on any grilled meat or poultry.

BARBECUE SAUCE

4	cups water
1/3	cup packed brown sugar
1/2	cup Worcestershire sauce
1/2	cup yellow mustard
2	cups ketchup
2	tablespoons red pepper flakes
1	cup cider vinegar
2	pork tenderloins (about 1½ pounds each)

Salt and freshly ground black pepper to taste

8 cups salad greens

To make the barbecue sauce: Combine all the ingredients in a stainless-steel stockpot and stir with a whisk until smooth. Bring to a boil over medium heat, reduce the heat to low, and simmer, stirring occasionally, for 30 minutes, or until the sauce is just slightly thickened. Set aside 1½ cups of sauce for this recipe. Refrigerate what you don't need in tightly sealed glass or plastic containers for up to 2 weeks.

Build a medium fire in a charcoal grill or heat a gas grill to 350°F. Sprinkle the pork tenderloins with salt and pepper. Oil the grill grate. Place the pork on the grate, cover the grill, and cook for 5 minutes on each side. Brush the tops liberally with the barbecue sauce, turn, and cook, uncovered, for 5 minutes. Brush the tops again with the barbecue sauce, turn, and cook, uncovered, for 5 more minutes, or until an instant-read thermometer inserted in the center of a tenderloin reaches 155°F. Transfer to a plate, cover loosely with aluminum foil, and let rest for about 10 minutes. Slice and serve atop the greens, drizzled with additional barbecue sauce.

Serves 8 to 10

Grilled Veggie-Pesto Wraps

In her classic *West Coast Cook Book,* published in 1952, Pasadena food editor Helen Brown boasts: "There's nothing dull about vegetable cookery on the West Coast. We have, and I do dare say it, the greatest variety of vegetables in the world, and we have most of them all year-round." For more than fifty years, California has led the nation in agricultural production. Progressive farmers in the valleys, foothills, coastal areas, and even the desert take advantage of the moderate Mediterranean climate to supply many U.S. markets with fresh vegetables of all kinds. Grilling brings out the flavor of just about every vegetable that's grown, and combining some in a warm tortilla makes a delightful lunch or light supper. Experiment with different vegetable combinations, and try different dressings, too. This filling also tastes great between two slices of sourdough bread. Serve warm, along with a bowl of olives and a sliced tomato salad.

VEGGIE MARINADE

½   cup olive oil

2   cloves garlic, minced

1   tablespoon fresh lemon juice

1   teaspoon dried tarragon

1   teaspoon dried thyme

Salt and freshly ground black pepper to taste

2   stalks celery, cut into 3-inch pieces

2   red bell peppers, or 1 red and 1 yellow bell pepper, seeded and cut into lengthwise strips about 2 inches wide

12   stalks asparagus

1   eggplant, cut into rounds about ¼-inch thick

2   portobello mushrooms

4   large flour tortillas

To make the marinade: Combine all the ingredients in a glass jar with a tight-fitting lid and shake until well blended. Arrange the celery, bell peppers, asparagus, eggplant, and mushrooms in sections on a large platter and drizzle with the marinade. Let sit for at least 30 minutes or up to 1 hour.

Build a medium fire in a charcoal grill or heat a gas grill to 350°F. Wrap the tortillas in aluminum foil.

To make the pesto dressing: Combine the basil, pecans, cheese, and garlic in a food processor. Pulse for several seconds until the basil is finely chopped. With the machine running, add the olive oil in a thin stream. With the machine off, use a rubber spatula to push all the basil on the sides of the bowl back down to the bottom. Pulse once again to blend evenly. Season with salt. Set aside.

When you're ready to cook, oil the grill grate. Place the tortilla bundle on one side of the grate. Begin roasting the vegetables by lifting them out of the marinade with tongs and arranging them together in sections on the grate or putting them into an oiled grill basket or on an oiled screen. Turn each section after it has cooked for 2 minutes. (If you wish, brush additional olive oil or any leftover marinade on the vegetables as they cook.) Cook for 4 to 8 minutes, or until lightly browned and showing light grill marks; the vegetables should just be starting to shrivel. Transfer the vegetables to the platter and cover loosely with aluminum foil to keep them warm. Unwrap the tortillas and place each directly on the grill. Sprinkle each with ¼ cup of the cheese, cover the grill, and heat through for about 1 minute, or until the cheese is just melted. Using tongs, transfer each tortilla to a serving plate. Top with some of the vegetables, spoon on a tablespoon or so of dressing, roll up, and serve.

Serves 4

PESTO DRESSING

2   **cups packed fresh basil leaves**
¼   **cup pecan halves**
¼   **cup grated Parmesan cheese**
2   **cloves garlic, coarsely chopped**
1   **cup olive oil**
Salt to taste

1   **cup (4 ounces) shredded Monterey Jack cheese**

Lamb Shoulder Chops with Cucumber-Yogurt Sauce

Starting in 1865, rail links between Colorado towns and markets to the east and west opened up new possibilities for ranchers to sell their beef to growing U.S. cities. But the state's lamb industry had an unplanned beginning. During the brutal winter of 1886–1887, a blizzard delayed the shipment of lambs from New Mexico to Nebraska. When the trains could run again in the spring, the lambs were too thin for the market and were sent on to Fort Collins to be fattened. Later sold for a profit in Chicago, they inspired the growth of a Colorado lamb industry. Today, this state ranks fifth in U.S. lamb production and is home to sixteen major lamb-processing plants. Most supermarkets sell a number of cuts, and lamb loins, butterflied legs, and chops are all delicious when grilled. This recipe uses lamb shoulder chops, sometimes called shoulder steaks, which are inexpensive (under $2 per pound) but very flavorful. They shrink when grilled, so allow 2 per person. Serve with Coleslaw (page 116) and Ranch Beans (page 119).

CUCUMBER-YOGURT SAUCE

1   cucumber, peeled, seeded, and diced

1   cup plain yogurt

2   cloves garlic, minced

Juice of ½ lemon (about 2 tablespoons)

1   tablespoon chopped fresh dill, or 1 teaspoon dried dill

1   tablespoon olive oil

Salt to taste

8   lamb shoulder chops (about 8 ounces each)

Four hours before grilling, make the cucumber-yogurt sauce: Combine all the ingredients in a small nonreactive bowl and stir gently to mix. Cover with plastic wrap and refrigerate.

Build a medium fire in a charcoal grill or heat a gas grill to 350°F. Oil the grill grate. Place the chops on the grate and cook for 4 minutes. Turn and cook 4 minutes longer, or until the chops are fork-tender and just starting to curl. Serve with a spoonful of sauce on the side.

Serves 4

New England Clambake

Despite the urban growth of its coastal cities, Connecticut has preserved great stretches of its rocky shoreline. The coastline's coves and bays include recreational shellfishing areas, where residents can harvest up to a half bushel of clams, mussels, and oysters per day. Catered clambakes are popular for weddings, company outings, and family reunions, and parks throughout the state provide designated clambake areas. Here's a quick and easy way to savor the succulent flavors of a traditional clambake, using a backyard grill rather than a fire at the beach. Prepare the lobster in advance, so all you have to do is reheat it on the grill. Serve with seafood cocktail sauce, rolls, and Coleslaw (page 116).

4	live lobsters (about 1 pound each)
4	to 6 ears fresh corn
4	pounds clams in the shell
4	pounds mussels in the shell
4	pounds oysters in the shell
½	cup (1 stick) butter

Fill a large stockpot three-fourths full with water and bring to a boil over high heat. Drop in 2 of the lobsters, head first, cover, and cook for 1 to 2 minutes, or just until they turn red. Remove with tongs and place in a large colander to cool and drain. Drop in the remaining 2 lobsters, and repeat. When cool to the touch, place them on a large cutting board. Remove the claws. Twist the tails off the bodies. Discard the bodies, or save for stock. With a large, sharp knife, cut each tail in half lengthwise, leaving the shell on. (To prepare ahead, cover with plastic wrap and refrigerate for up to 8 hours.)

Two to 4 hours before grilling, grasp each ear of corn and gently pull down the husks, exposing just enough of the kernels to make it possible to pull off all the silk, or as much as

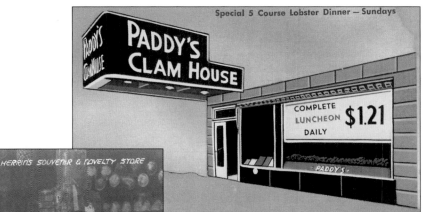

Special 5 Course Lobster Dinner — Sundays

PADDY'S CLAM HOUSE

PADDY'S CLAM HOUSE

COMPLETE LUNCHEON **$1.21** DAILY

PADDY'S·

HERRIN'S SOUVENIR & NOVELTY STORE

GIANT MAN-EATING CLAM From South Seas. APPROXIMATE WEIGHT 400 lb. 36 in. ACROSS OVER 150 YEARS OLD

few minutes with tongs, for 10 to 12 minutes, or until the husks are slightly backened and you can smell roasted corn. Transfer the corn to a large bowl and cover loosely with aluminum foil.

Reduce the heat in a gas grill to 350°F. Rinse the clams and mussels in a large colander and discard any that have opened or have cracked shells. Scrub the oysters with a stiff brush and add to the colander. Melt the butter in a small saucepan over low heat. Put the lobster tails, shell side down, and the claws on the grill and cook for 3 minutes. Brush the tail pieces with butter, turn along with the claws, and cook for 3 minutes longer. Using tongs, transfer the lobster pieces to a large platter and cover loosely with aluminum foil. Place the clams and mussels on the grill grate, cover, and cook for 5 minutes. Discard any that do not open. Heap the clams and mussels onto a platter. Place the oysters on the grate and cook for about 3 minutes, or until the shells just begin to open and the juice bubbles and starts to dribble out. Using tongs, turn them over and cook for about 3 minutes longer, or until the shells open. Arrange the oysters on a platter, remove the foil from the lobster, and invite your guests to dig in. Pour the remaining melted butter into 4 small ramekins for dipping.

possible. Pull the husks back up to cover the ear, then strip off the toughest outer husks, leaving each ear covered with several layers of the lighter green inner husks. Look through the discarded outer husks and find the longest ones. Rip 12 thin lengthwise strips from these husks and tie one around the tip of each ear to hold the husks in place. (The fresher the corn, the easier it will be to tie it; you only need to loop one end around the other, not make a bow.) Put the corn in a large stockpot, cover with cold water, and soak for 2 to 4 hours.

Build a medium-hot fire in a charcoal grill or heat a gas grill to 375°F. Remove the corn from the water and shake it gently to get rid of excess water. Oil the grill grate, add the corn, and cook, turning the ears every

Serves 4 to 6

Apricot Duck Kabobs

Greetings from DELAWARE

With its long stretches of marshland and bay, Delaware became known as a great place for duck hunting in the late 1800s, and remained so through the 1940s. Before dredging operations and industrial pollution destroyed the native habitats, wild rice that grew in the tidal wetlands attracted large numbers of migrating birds. In 1980, a program called Delaware Ducks Unlimited was launched to raise funds for waterfowl conservation and improve waterfowl habitats. To date, twenty-five of the state's waterfowl species have appeared on annual stamps, which waterfowl hunters are required to purchase and display during the state's fall and winter duck season. Luckily, you don't need to wait until then to serve duck at a cookout. Ducks are readily available fresh or frozen; check labels to find a cruelty-free producer. Serve with Tabbouleh (page 116).

4	boneless, skinless duck breast fillets (4 to 6 ounces each)
2	tablespoons olive oil
2	tablespoons white balsamic vinegar
⅓	cup dry white wine
⅓	cup apricot jam (preferably fruit-only, without added sugar)
4	fresh apricots, halved and pitted
3	red bell peppers, or a mixture of red, yellow, and orange bell peppers, seeded and cut into 1-inch squares

The night before grilling, cut the duck into 1-inch cubes. (Don't worry if you end up with some bits of meat; save all the pieces.) Combine the olive oil, vinegar, wine, and jam in a medium nonreactive bowl and stir with a whisk until smooth. Add the duck pieces and toss gently with a rubber spatula until well coated. Cover with plastic wrap and refrigerate overnight.

Soak 8 long wooden skewers in water to cover for 30 minutes. Build a medium-hot fire in a charcoal grill or heat a gas grill to 375°F. Thread the skewers, alternating 4 to 5 duck pieces with apricot and bell pepper pieces. Space the pieces so they aren't touching, to allow for even cooking. Bring the remaining

marinade to a boil and brush it on the skewers.
Oil the grill grate, add the skewers, and cook
for a total of 8 minutes, turning the skewers
every 2 minutes, or until the duck is browned
and the peppers and apricots are just starting
to shrivel.

Using a fork, slide the kabob pieces off the
skewers onto dinner plates and serve
with tabbouleh.

Serves 4

MISSISSIPPI · ALA · MISS · Mobile · Tallahassee

Greetings from FLORIDA

Sunny South

Grilled Grouper with Strawberry-Lime Relish

A member of the sea bass family and one of the state's most important commercial fish, the grouper is an aggressive fighter sought offshore by anglers who hope to land specimens weighing thirty pounds or more. Charter boats drift bait a foot or so off the bottom of the ocean, or put out lines for slow trolling. Most plentiful in Florida markets during late spring and summer, fresh grouper is available locally throughout the year. It's a lean, low-fat fish, best cooked skinned. Be sure to oil both the grill grate and the fish before you start cooking to keep it from sticking to the grate. Serve with couscous and a spinach salad. If you can't find grouper, substitute another firm-fleshed white fish such as haddock, hake, snapper, tilefish, or wolffish.

STRAWBERRY-LIME RELISH

2	cups fresh strawberries, hulled and diced
1	tablespoon minced fresh mint, or 1 teaspoon dried mint
2	tablespoons fresh lime juice
1	tablespoon packed brown sugar
½	teaspoon red pepper flakes (optional)
6	boneless, skinless grouper fillets (6 to 8 ounces each)
1	tablespoon olive oil
1	tablespoon fresh lime juice

To make the strawberry-lime relish: Combine all the ingredients in a medium nonreactive bowl and toss gently with a rubber spatula. Let the mixture sit at room temperature for 1 to 2 hours, stirring occasionally, to let the flavors blend.

Build a medium-hot fire in a charcoal grill or heat a gas grill to 375°F. Arrange the fillets on a large platter. Combine the olive oil and lime juice in a small nonreactive bowl and brush the mixture on both sides of the fillets. Oil the grill grate, add the fillets, and cook for 4 minutes on each side, or until the fish is opaque throughout. Put each piece on a dinner plate and spoon some of the relish over the top.

Serves 6

MANATEE MANATEE
COUNTY COUNTY
florida *florida*

K4

"*Supplies the Market Basket of the Nation*"

Grilled Vidalia Onions

A farmers' market built in Vidalia in the 1940s launched the popularity of the region's legendary sweet onions. Today, they are grown in twenty counties in the state. In 1990, the Vidalia onion became Georgia's official state vegetable. Crops are harvested from late April to mid-June, but the large, light-brown onions with bright-white insides are sold in supermarkets nationwide through December. Eaten raw, Vidalias are juicy and mild. Grilling brings out their sweetness. Toss a few over hot coals the next time you cook anything. They're a treat on top of hamburgers, or served with steaks or chicken. Sprinkle them with your favorite salad dressing and add them to a green salad, or use them to add a special flavor to Grilled Tomato–Bread Salad (page 82).

2 large Vidalia onions (about 1½ pounds total), cut into ¼-inch-thick slices

3 tablespoons olive oil

Build a medium fire in a charcoal grill or heat a gas grill to 350°F. Lay the onion slices on a baking sheet and brush the tops with the olive oil. Oil the grill grate and add the onion slices, oiled side down. Cook for about 3 minutes, or until some of the rings begin to brown. As the onions cook, brush the tops with olive oil. Carefully turn with a spatula, keeping all the rings intact, and cook for another 3 minutes, or until the onions soften. Using the spatula, gently slide them off the grill and onto a serving tray.

Serves 4 to 6

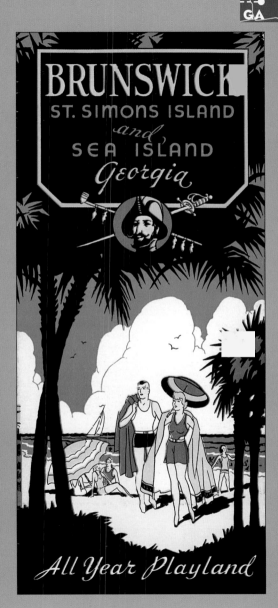

Festival Pineapple

If you visit Hawaii, you'll eventually encounter a luau. The word literally refers to young taro leaves, which are often wrapped around chicken or seafood and then baked, but it has come to represent the ultimate outdoor, multicourse feast, with a slow-cooked kalua pig as the main attraction. Pineapple, one of the state's signature products, is always part of the feast in some form. It's also grilled and presented in a number of desserts at Lana'i City's annual pineapple festival in July. Hawaii's first commercial pineapple plantation was established in Oahu in 1885, and the state led world production into the early 1960s. (If you live in the continental United States, the pineapple you bring home today is probably from Thailand, the Philippines, Brazil, Central America, or Mexico; you can order Hawaiian pineapples online.) Remember to always sniff a pineapple before you buy it in the store; it should smell slightly sweet. Here's a quick and easy way to put a traditional taste of Hawaii on your table.

2	ripe pineapples
2	tablespoons fresh lemon or lime juice
2	tablespoons packed brown sugar

Build a medium fire in a charcoal grill or heat a gas grill to 350°F. Keeping the leaves and peel on the pineapples, slice each one in half lengthwise with a large knife, cutting cleanly right through the leaves so they remain attached. Cut each half again lengthwise, making 4 wedges, with a bit of the leaves attached to each wedge. Combine the lemon juice and brown sugar in a small nonreactive bowl and stir until smooth. Brush some of the sugar mixture on the cut sides of the wedges. Oil the grill grate and add the pineapple wedges,

placing one face of the cut side down. Cook
for about 4 minutes on each face of the cut
side, or until the glaze sizzles. Serve hot on
large plates.

Serves 8

Crispy Idaho Potato Wedges

It's no surprise that Idaho is home to the country's only potato museum. The Idaho Potato Exposition in Blackfoot even promises "Free Taters for Out-of-Staters," and comes through by serving each qualified visitor a hot baked potato, slathered with butter and sour cream. Potatoes and the state of Idaho have gone together in cooks' minds since the late 1800s, when the "Grown in Idaho" label was first proudly affixed to shipments of Russet Burbank, the gold-standard variety that cooks up light and fluffy, retains little oil when fried, and can be stored for months. Bake the potatoes for this recipe in advance (up to 24 hours before mealtime), and put them on the grill along with steaks, burgers, or fish. The mustard caramelizes as they cook, giving them a crisp texture as well as a spicy flavor.

- 2   large Idaho russet potatoes (12 to 14 ounces each)
- ½   cup Dijon mustard
- 2   tablespoons olive oil
- 1   tablespoon minced fresh thyme, or 1 teaspoon dried thyme

Coarse salt and freshly ground black pepper to taste

An hour before grilling, heat the oven to 400°F. Scrub the potatoes and prick in several places with a fork. Place directly on the oven rack and bake for about 40 minutes, or until they give a bit when pressed but are not soft throughout. Let cool for about 15 minutes. (If baking them 1 day ahead, refrigerate them after they have cooled completely.) With a large knife, slice each potato into 4 lengthwise wedges.

Nelson's Cafe
and
Pilots Club

BURLEY
IDAHO

Build a medium fire in a charcoal grill or heat a gas grill to 350°F. Combine the mustard, olive oil, thyme, salt, and pepper in a large nonreactive bowl. Add the potato wedges and toss gently to coat with the mustard mixture. Oil the grill grate. Using tongs, arrange the wedges on the grate. Cover the grill and cook the wedges, turning every 5 minutes, for about 15 minutes, or until tender and evenly browned. Serve hot or warm.

Serves 4

BIG ATTRACTIONS IN
ILLINOIS

Roasted Corn

Famous for its miles of cornfields, Illinois produces about 1.87 billion bushels of corn annually, ranking second to Iowa in the U.S. production of this important crop. In 1922, Secretary of Agriculture Henry Wallace organized a corn-husking contest in Illinois and today the tradition continues in Roseville at the Annual Illinois State Cornhusking Contest, where challengers wearing a leather wrist wrap and thumb hook compete to be the fastest at hooking ears from the stalks, husking them, and flipping them into a wagon. If you've ever found it tedious to shuck corn, consider that champion huskers can throw fifty to sixty ears a minute. However many ears you're confronting, try grilling them for a whole new taste. While the freshest corn is always the best, this method restores flavor to ears that have spent a few days in the refrigerator.

12 ears unshucked corn
Butter, salt, and freshly ground
    black pepper for serving

Two to 4 hours before grilling, grasp each ear and gently pull down the husks, exposing just enough of the kernels to make it possible to pull off all the silk, or as much as possible. Pull the husks back up to cover the ear, then strip off the toughest outer husks, leaving each ear covered with several layers of the lighter green inner husks. Look through the discarded outer husks and find the longest ones. Rip 12 thin lengthwise strips from these husks and tie one around the tip of each ear to hold the husks in place. (The fresher the corn, the easier it will be to tie it; you only need to loop one end around the other, not make a bow.) Put the corn in a large stockpot, cover with cold water, and soak for 2 to 4 hours.

Build a medium-hot fire in a charcoal grill or heat a gas grill to 375°F. Remove the corn from the water and shake it gently to get rid of excess water. Oil the grill grate, add the corn, and cook, turning the ears every few minutes with tongs, for 10 to 12 minutes, or until the husks are slightly blackened and you can smell roasted corn. Serve with butter, salt, and pepper.

Serves 8 to 12

Greetings from INDIANA

Beer Can Chicken

Tailgating, the ultimate parking lot cookout, is a serious passion for Indiana residents, whether they're cheering the professional NFL Colts, or college teams such as the Indiana University Hoosiers, the Purdue Boilermakers, or Notre Dame's Fighting Irish. A recent study shows that nearly half of the country's tailgaters spend $500 or more per season on food and supplies. (To learn more about tailgating, visit www.tailgatershandbook.com.) The unusual recipe below has been popular on the tailgating circuit for several years, especially with Colts fans. (You can also buy a Keg Roaster, which comes with metal sleeves to hold beer cans in place for several chickens, and a domed lid to seal in the heat. Visit www.campchef.com for details.) This recipe is great fun to prepare for family reunions, and the meat makes terrific cold sandwiches. It goes nicely with Mom's Potato Salad (page 117) and New England Baked Beans (page 120). Most grills can cook at least four upright chickens at a time. Shop for those under 4 pounds; the bigger birds can get tippy.

2   cups aromatic wood chips

One 12-ounce can beer

6   teaspoons Rib Rub (page 62) or commercial spice rub

1   whole chicken (3½ to 4 pounds), patted dry with paper towels

Put the wood chips in a bucket and add water to cover. Remove the tab from the beer can. Using a beer-can opener, make a few more holes in the top of the can. Pour half the beer into the bucket of wood chips. Soak the chips for 1 hour. Set the half-filled can of beer aside.

Build a medium indirect fire, using a drip pan, in a charcoal grill, or heat a gas grill to 350°F and prepare it for indirect heat using a drip pan (see page 11). Sprinkle 1 teaspoon of the Rib Rub inside the body cavity of the chicken and another 1 teaspoon inside the neck cavity. Rub the bird all over on the outside with

2 teaspoons of the rub. Spoon the remaining 2 teaspoons rub through the holes into the beer in the can. (It will foam up a bit.) Insert the beer can, open side up, into the chicken's body cavity and spread out the legs to form a sort of tripod. (The beer can will hold the chicken upright as it cooks.) Fold the wing tips akimbo and tuck behind the chicken's back.

Drain the wood chips. If using a charcoal grill, toss the chips on the coals. For a gas grill, see page 9. Stand the chicken up in the center of the hot grate, over the drip pan. Cover the grill and cook the chicken for 1¼ to 1½ hours, or until the skin is very crisp, dark golden brown and the meat is opaque throughout; an instant-read thermometer inserted in the breast should read 180°F. Replenish the coals every 30 to 40 minutes.

Using tongs, carefully transfer the chicken in its upright position on the beer can to a platter and present it to your guests. Let the chicken rest for 5 minutes. Then, holding the base of the beer can with an oven mitt, carefully lift the chicken off the beer can with tongs. Take care not to spill the hot beer. Carve the chicken and serve.

Serves 4 to 6

39

Fruit-Stuffed Iowa Chops with Apple-Pecan Sauce

Iowa tops the list as the country's largest pork producer. The state boasts five hogs for every person, with close to 28 million animals processed in the state each year. With increasing consumer demand for sound animal husbandry and top flavor, a number of the state's farmers have turned their attention to raising heirloom breeds such as Berkshire, Kurobuta, and Duroc. (To learn more about the many such farms in Iowa and throughout the United States, visit www.nichepork.org.) This recipe highlights pork at its very best: grilled with a surprise on the inside, and served with an apple-based sauce, the perfect complement.

1½ cups apple cider
1 tablespoon honey
4 cloves garlic, crushed
4 pork chops, 1¼ to 1½ inches thick

APPLE-PECAN SAUCE
1 cup applesauce with cinnamon
¼ cup finely chopped pecans
½ cup Amaretto liqueur
1 cup finely chopped fresh strawberries or cherries or a combination

The night before grilling, combine the cider and honey in a small nonreactive bowl. Blend with a whisk for about 1 minute, or until the honey is completely dissolved. Add the garlic to the cider and honey mixture. Cut a deep pocket, about 2 inches long, in the side of each chop. Place the pork chops in a heavy resealable plastic bag and

World's Largest Pecan

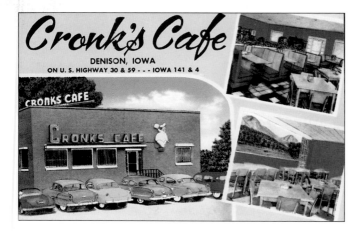

Cronk's Cafe
DENISON, IOWA
ON U. S. HIGHWAY 30 & 59 - - - IOWA 141 & 4

pour in the cider mixture. Seal and refrigerate for 24 hours, laying the bag flat to ensure that the meat is well covered.

Build a medium fire in a charcoal grill or heat a gas grill to 350°F.

To make the apple-pecan sauce: Combine the applesauce, pecans, Amaretto, and ½ cup of the chopped fruit in a small saucepan. Bring to a boil, reduce the heat to low, and simmer for about 5 minutes, or until the sauce is slightly thickened and the Amaretto flavor is well blended with the other ingredients. Remove from the heat and set aside.

Remove the chops from the marinade. Using a teaspoon, stuff the pockets in the chops with the remaining chopped fruit. Close each pocket with a toothpick. Reheat the sauce and keep warm. Oil the grill grate and add the chops. Cover the grill and cook the chops for 7 to 10 minutes on each side, or until lightly browned and fork-tender. Serve immediately, with the warm sauce spooned on top.

Serves 4

THE IOWA GREAT LAKES

AMERICA'S MOST BEAUTIFUL BLUE WATER LAKES

KSU Barbecued Chicken

From 1946 to 1951, the Atlantic and Pacific Tea Company (A&P) sponsored the Chicken of Tomorrow Contest, a state-level program designed to encourage the breeding of chickens for superior meat. Kansas participated in the event every year, and today Kansas breeders are known nationally for their meaty White Wyandotte and Buff Brahma chickens. As shown by the Kansas State Fair exhibits, many other breeds—large birds such as Rhode Island Reds, Crested Polish, and Black Australorps, as well as bantams—are still being raised throughout the state by small farmers, many of them 4-H kids.

Barbecued chicken is popular cookout fare in Kansas, where half chickens are often served for family reunions, office parties, and charity events. Here's the official recipe for chicken halves used by the Kansas State University Animal Sciences and Industry Department. For big feeds, they recommend using a barbecue pit made from a metal drum cut in half and designed to keep the cooking surface 20 to 24 inches from the fire. (To obtain complete details on constructing a pit, and on cooking chicken for up to 250 people, visit www.oznet.ksu.edu/library, and search under "barbecuing chicken.") The following recipe has been adapted for backyard grills by precooking the chickens and then finishing them off over the coals. Serve with hot rolls, baked beans, cottage cheese, and coleslaw.

2	small chickens (3½ to 4 pounds each)
2	teaspoons salt

KSU BARBECUE SAUCE

2	tablespoons butter or vegetable oil
1	cup water
½	cup malt or cider vinegar
1½	teaspoons Worcestershire sauce
1½	teaspoons Tabasco sauce
¾	teaspoon dry mustard
1	tablespoon sugar

Thirty minutes before grilling, heat the oven to 400°F. Put the chickens on a cutting board and, using a large knife, split them lengthwise into halves. Press down on them gently to flatten slightly. Arrange the chicken halves in a large baking dish, breast side up, and sprinkle with 1 teaspoon of the salt. Bake for 30 minutes, turning the halves after 15 minutes and sprinkling them with the remaining 1 teaspoon salt. (To make ahead, let cool and refrigerate for up to 24 hours.)

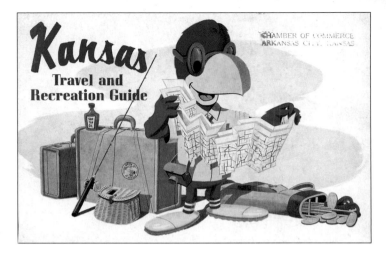

Build a low fire in a charcoal grill or heat a gas grill to 325°F.

To make the barbecue sauce: Combine the butter, water, vinegar, Worcestershire sauce, and Tabasco sauce in a medium nonreactive saucepan. Bring to a boil over medium-hot heat. Combine all the remaining ingredients in a small bowl and whisk them into the boiling liquid. Reduce the heat to low and simmer, stirring occasionally, for 20 minutes, or until the sauce is reduced to about ½ cup.

Oil the grill grate and add the chickens, breast side up. Brush with the barbecue sauce and cook, turning and basting with sauce every 5 minutes, for 30 minutes, or until the juices run clear when you pierce the skin with a fork or an instant-read thermometer registers 180°F when inserted in the breast. Serve immediately, on large plates.

Serves 4

½   **teaspoon salt**

½   **teaspoon chili powder**

½   **teaspoon freshly ground black pepper**

½   **teaspoon Hungarian paprika**

½   **teaspoon onion powder**

⅛   **teaspoon garlic powder**

259

Louisville

Greetings from
KENTUCKY
SCENIC
ROMANTIC, HISTORIC

Bourbon-Marinated Sirloin

During the nineteenth century, barrels of whiskey made throughout Kentucky and shipped down the Ohio and Mississippi rivers to New Orleans were often stamped *Bourbon,* indicating that they had come through Bourbon County. In the heart of its Blue Grass Country, Kentucky currently makes 90 percent of the world's bourbon. In Bardstown, the annual Kentucky Bourbon Festival in September gives residents a chance to celebrate their bourbon-making tradition, which began in 1776. The caramel-and-vanilla-tasting spirits with a hint of charcoal are made by distilling grain, which by law must include at least 51 percent corn, and must be aged for at least two years in charred oak barrels. While it's pleasant for sipping, bourbon also makes a fine ingredient in a marinade for meat, giving steak a juicy sweetness when grilled. Serve with a green salad and sliced ripe tomatoes.

⅓ cup Kentucky bourbon (Jim Beam, Four Roses, Maker's Mark, or Wild Turkey)

⅓ cup soy sauce

3 cloves garlic, minced

2 pounds beef sirloin steak, 1 to 1½ inches thick

Four hours before grilling, combine the bourbon, soy sauce, and garlic in a shallow nonreactive dish and stir with a whisk to blend. Put the steak on top of the marinade, turn once, cover with plastic wrap, and refrigerate for 4 hours, turning once after about 2 hours. Remove the steak from the refrigerator 30 minutes before grilling.

KENTUCKY PARKS

Build a medium-hot fire in a charcoal grill or heat a gas grill to 375°F. Oil the grill grate. Using tongs, remove the steak from the marinade and place it on the grate. Discard the marinade. Cook the steak, turning once with tongs, about 6 minutes on each side for medium-rare or 8 minutes on each side for medium. Transfer the steak to a cutting board and slice it diagonally across the grain.

Serves 4

Grilled Cajun Shrimp

When Acadians from Canada traveled south to settle in the southern Louisiana countryside during the eighteenth century, they launched the tradition of cooking well-seasoned meat and seafood, and serving it with rice. Spicy shrimp became one of their signature dishes. With its long coastline and abundant estuaries and marshes

Louisiana is the nation's number-one producer of shrimp. Today, in the heart of Cajun country, the Louisiana Shrimp and Petroleum Festival honors the workers of these two important local industries. Serve this delicious low-carb dish spiced with Cajun seasoning as an appetizer, or with rice and sliced tomatoes as a main course.

1	teaspoon chili powder
½	tablespoon Hungarian paprika
1	teaspoon garlic powder
1	teaspoon onion powder
¼	teaspoon freshly ground black pepper
½	teaspoon cayenne pepper
½	teaspoon dried oregano
½	teaspoon dried thyme
2	tablespoons fresh lemon juice
1	to 1¼ pounds (30 to 36) large shrimp, shelled and deveined

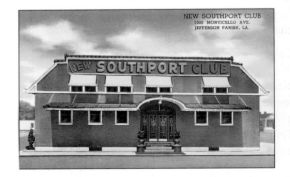

NEW SOUTHPORT CLUB
1300 MONTICELLO AVE.
JEFFERSON PARISH, LA.

The New Orleans
VISITOR'S GUIDE

Visitors
City Guide

Soak 6 long wooden skewers in water to cover
for 30 minutes. Build a medium fire in a
charcoal grill or heat a gas grill to 350°F.

Combine the spices and herbs in a medium
nonreactive bowl and stir with a whisk until
blended. Add the lemon juice and whisk for a
few seconds until smooth. Add the shrimp and
gently toss in the mixture until well coated.
Thread 5 or 6 shrimp onto each of the skewers
and arrange on a large platter.

Oil the grate, add the skewers, and cook for
1½ minutes on each side, or until evenly pink.
Don't overcook, or the shrimp will become
tough. Serve immediately.

Serves 4 to 6

Grilled Lobster

Maine's rocky coastline and cold, clean waters provide ideal conditions for lobster. For decades, this hauntingly delicious crustacean has played an important role in the state's economy and identity. In 1840, Maine began marketing canned lobster and shipping it as far as California. In 1880, prices reached 2 cents a pound. Although you'll pay at least four hundred times that today, whether you buy from a fishmonger, a supermarket, or online, lobster remains a treat worthy of special meals, even wedding feasts. Although commonly boiled or steamed, it acquires special flavor when grilled. Serve with Roasted Corn (page 36).

4   **live Maine lobsters (1 to 1¼ pounds each)**

½   **cup (1 stick) butter**

Juice of 1 lemon (about ¼ cup; optional)

Fill a large stockpot three-fourths full with water and bring to a boil over high heat. Drop in 2 of the lobsters, head first, cover, and cook for 1 to 2 minutes, or just until they turn red. Remove with tongs and place in a large colander to cool and drain. Drop in the remaining 2

THE LOBSTER TRAP — LINCOLNVILLE BEACH, MAINE   B288

lobsters, and repeat. When cool to the touch, place them on a large cutting board. Remove the claws. Twist the tails off the bodies. Discard the bodies, or save for stock. With a large, sharp knife cut each tail in half lengthwise, leaving the shell on. (To prepare ahead, cover with plastic wrap and refrigerate for up to 8 hours.)

Build a medium fire in a charcoal grill or heat a gas grill to 350°F. Melt the butter in a small nonreactive saucepan over low heat and whisk in the lemon juice, if using. Oil the grill grate and add the lobster tails, shell side down, and the claws. Cook for 3 minutes, brush the tail pieces with the butter, turn along with the claws, and cook 3 minutes longer, or until the flesh is opaque throughout. Using tongs, transfer the lobster pieces to a large platter. Serve hot, with the remaining melted butter mixture.

Serves 4

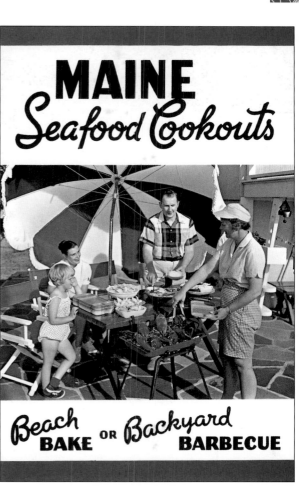

MAINE
Seafood Cookouts

Beach BAKE OR *Backyard* BARBECUE

Grilled Soft-Shell Crabs

Maryland has an official state crustacean, the blue crab, which thrives in Chesapeake Bay, where estuaries and rivers give this small state one of the longest waterfronts. With their likenesses proudly worn on T-shirts and sweatshirts, and sold on souvenir mugs and magnets, crabs are popular fare at local crab houses, where they are steamed and served with mallets for cracking them open. The blue crab is especially beloved from May through September, when it sheds its hard outer shell and becomes a soft-shell crab that is entirely edible. These are delicious grilled, and best served simply. The males, or "jimmies," have the most meat. Buy them live or look for them frozen and thaw before proceeding. (If you need to clean them yourself, use a pair of kitchen shears and make a straight cut about ¼ inch behind the eyes and mouth, removing both. Twist or cut off the small flap, or apron, on the crab's underside, then gently lift off the top shell and snip out the lungs on each side.) Serve with French bread and Coleslaw (page 116).

1	cup olive oil
3	tablespoons white balsamic vinegar
1	tablespoon fresh lemon juice
1	teaspoon hot sauce
½	teaspoon salt
½	teaspoon dried tarragon
12	soft-shell crabs, about 3 to 4 inches across

In a small nonreactive bowl, combine the olive oil, vinegar, lemon juice, hot sauce, salt, and tarragon and blend with a whisk until smooth. Let the marinade sit at room temperature for 2 to 3 hours to allow the flavors to blend.

Build a medium fire in a charcoal grill or heat a gas grill to 350°F. Place the crabs in a large, shallow nonreactive bowl and pour the marinade over them. Let stand at room temperature for 10 to 15 minutes. Remove the crabs from the marinade. Bring the marinade to a boil over medium heat in a small saucepan, simmer for 5 minutes, remove from the heat, and set aside.

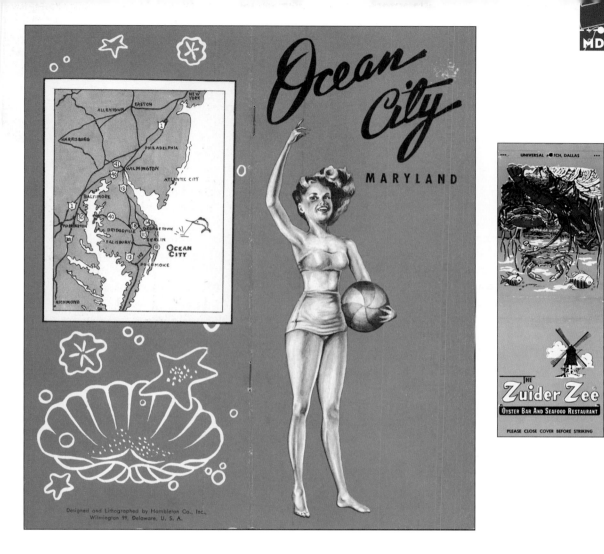

Oil the grill grate. Using tongs, add the crabs. Brush the tops with the marinade. Cover the grill and cook for 4 minutes. Turn the crabs over, brush with the marinade, cover the grill, and cook 4 minutes longer, or until the crabs turn a reddish brown.

Using tongs, arrange the cooked crabs in several rows on a large platter or heap them into a large serving bowl and pass them around the table.

Serves 4 to 6

Greetings from MASSACHUSETTS

Smoked Turkey

It was common practice for the Massachusetts Bay colonists to set aside a day for prayer and thanks, but Gov. William Bradford's call for thanks in Plymouth in 1621, and the three-day feast that followed, has become a legendary event. In 1863, Pres. Abraham Lincoln declared Thanksgiving a national holiday.

Knowing how to cook a whole turkey on your grill is a useful skill at holiday time, since it leaves the oven free for vegetable side dishes and pies. It's also the making of a great summer feast, as it feeds a gang and there's usually some left over for sandwiches. From Memorial Day to the Fourth of July, poultry purveyors clean out their inventories and frozen turkey prices plummet, making it an economical choice for a big gathering, served with New England Baked Beans (page 120) and Mom's Potato Salad (page 117). Since no one wants to crank up the oven during hot weather, this grilling alternative makes great sense. The recipe below includes instructions for brining a turkey, which simply means that you let it soak in a seasoned liquid for a day before cooking. The process makes the meat juicy and tender. This is an optional step, but one that's highly recommended for frozen supermarket turkeys that can otherwise deliver dry and lackluster results. You can put a frozen turkey in the brine, but it will take two or three hours longer to thaw completely.

BRINE

½ cup salt

½ cup honey

½ cup white wine vinegar or
    cider vinegar

3 tablespoons Worcestershire sauce

1 tablespoon Dijon mustard

1 teaspoon quatre épices
    (four-spice blend)

4 cups water, plus more as needed

3 bay leaves

2 onions, diced

4 cloves garlic, smashed

One 10- to 12-pound turkey, giblets removed

Salt and freshly ground black pepper to taste

Olive oil for coating

½ cup hickory or mesquite chips

A day before grilling, make the turkey brine, if using: Combine the salt, honey, vinegar, Worcestershire sauce, mustard, and quatre épices in a small nonreactive bowl and stir with a whisk until smooth. Pour 2 cups of the water into a stainless-steel or enameled pot large enough to hold the turkey, add the honey mixture, and stir with a whisk until blended. Add the remaining 2 cups water, along with all the remaining ingredients. Lower the turkey into the brine. Add more water until the turkey is completely submerged. Cover the top of the pot with a lid or plastic wrap and refrigerate for at least 8 hours or overnight.

Remove the turkey from the brine and pat it dry. Season the cavity with salt and pepper and coat the skin with olive oil. On the counter, lay out a sheet of aluminum foil, shiny side up, approximately 2½ times the turkey's length. Grease the entire length of foil with olive oil. Place the turkey, breast side up, lengthwise on the foil and fold up the foil to wrap the turkey well, overlapping and folding the edges of foil

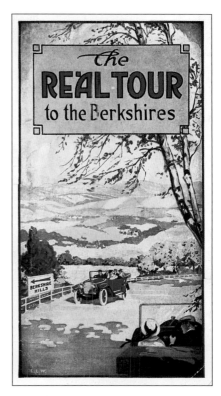

together to seal over the breast side (top). Gently press the foil against the wings and legs, making sure the tips of the wings don't puncture the foil. Pull off one more piece of foil about the same length and stretch it out on the counter, shiny side up. Center the turkey on it widthwise, bring up the foil as before, and fold it over the breast section. Be sure the turkey is completely covered with foil. Use another piece if necessary.

Build a medium indirect fire with the coals in a ring in a charcoal grill using a drip pan or heat a gas grill to 350°F and prepare it for indirect heat using a drip pan (see page 11). Place 2 bricks, flat side down, side by side in the center of the ring. These will help radiate even heat. Set the grate on the grill. Adjust the air vents to half-open.

Place the foil-wrapped turkey on the grate directly above the bricks, cover the grill, and open the lid air vent just over halfway. Cook

for about 2 hours, adding more coals every 30 to 45 minutes as necessary to keep the ring burning evenly. Put the wood chips in water to cover and let them soak.

After 2 hours, remove the grill cover. Wearing oven mitts, lift off the grate, being careful not to let the turkey tumble off. (Set it down on 2 bricks on the ground or another surface that won't be damaged by heat and grease stains.) Drain the wood chips. If using a charcoal grill, sprinkle them over the ring of coals; if using a gas grill, see page 9. Add more coals if necessary to keep the fire going for up to 1 more hour.

Starting with the piece over the breast, peel the foil way from the turkey, being careful not to remove any turkey skin. Use a small, sharp knife to loosen the foil if necessary. Leave a "tray" of foil around the bottom of the turkey. With a bulb baster, remove any juices that have accumulated in the tray. Place the grill grate and turkey back over the coals and cover the grill. Adjust the lid vents to be about one-fourth open and cook 30 to 60 minutes longer, or until the turkey's legs wiggle freely and the breast meat registers 180°F on an instant-read thermometer.

With the bulb baster, siphon off any accumulated juices in the foil tray. Insert a barbecue fork into the turkey's cavity and lift it onto a platter, gently pulling off the remaining aluminum foil before you set it down. Cover the turkey loosely with clean foil and let it sit for 20 minutes before carving.

Serves 8 to 10

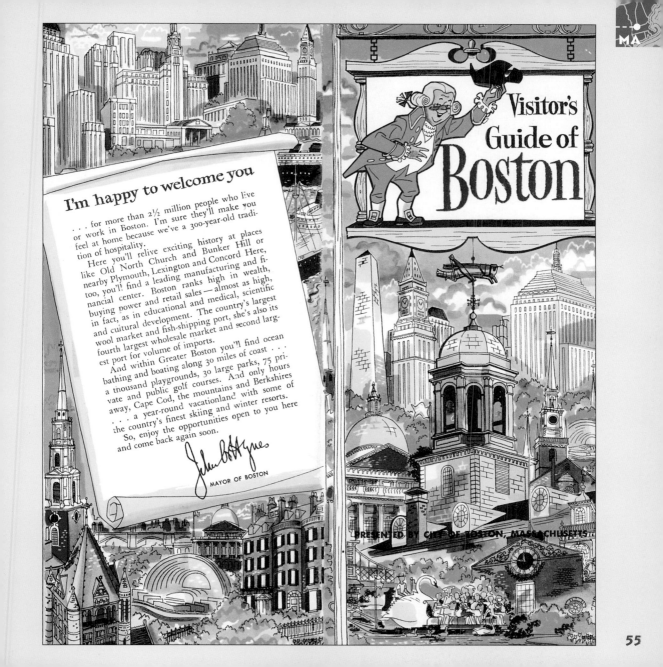

Visitor's Guide of Boston

I'm happy to welcome you

. . . for more than 2½ million people who live or work in Boston. I'm sure they'll make you feel at home because we've a 300-year-old tradition of hospitality.

Here you'll relive exciting history at places like Old North Church and Bunker Hill or nearby Plymouth, Lexington and Concord Here, too, you'll find a leading manufacturing and financial center. Boston ranks high in wealth, buying power and retail sales — almost as high, in fact, as in educational and medical, scientific and cultural development. The country's largest wool market and fish-shipping port, she's also its fourth largest wholesale market and second largest port for volume of imports.

And within Greater Boston you'll find ocean bathing and boating along 30 miles of coast . . . a thousand playgrounds, 30 large parks, 75 private and public golf courses. And only hours away, Cape Cod, the mountains and Berkshires . . . a year-round vacationland with some of the country's finest skiing and winter resorts.

So, enjoy the opportunities open to you here and come back again soon.

John B. Hynes

MAYOR OF BOSTON

PRESENTED BY CITY OF BOSTON, MASSACHUSETTS

Cherry Burgers

Michigan lawmakers are working on a wonderful thing—an official state burger—which means that cherry burgers may one day have a place right up there with the state bird (robin), state fish (brook trout), and state flower (apple blossom). Making good use of local tart cherries, an industry that developed in Lake Michigan orchards in the early 1900s, sausage maker Ray Pleva, a native of Cedar, Michigan, created the cherry burger by grinding cherries together with beef. Patented in 1995 as Plevalean, the mixture is sold in a number of supermarkets and can also be ordered online. It's served in schools in seventeen states as well. And it's serious business. A study by scientists at Michigan State University shows that adding cherries to ground beef substantially reduces the formation of potentially carcinogenic compounds that can form when meat is grilled, especially when it is blackened. Plevalean makes a moist and juicy burger with a great taste. If you don't have any on hand, try this improvised method for making your own mixture. Serve it in sesame seed buns with all the fixings and wait for the response.

⅓   cup fresh tart cherries, pitted

1   pound lean ground beef

4   hamburger buns

Mustard, ketchup, and relish
    for serving

Build a medium-hot fire in a charcoal grill or heat a gas grill to 375°F. Put the cherries in a food processor and process for 1 minute, or until the cherries are well chopped and very juicy. Add the ground beef and pulse for several seconds until the cherries are well mixed into the meat. With clean hands, shape the meat into 4 patties no more than ½ inch thick.

Oil the grill grate, add the patties, and cook, turning once and watching carefully that they do not burn, for 4 to 6 minutes per side for

medium. If they start to darken, move them
to the cooler outer edges of the grate.

Serve immediately in the buns, with mustard,
ketchup, and relish.

Serves 4

Variation: If you can't find fresh tart cherries,
substitute dried tart cherries and add 2 tablespoons of water when you put them in the
food processor.

Grilled Steak with Peach Salsa

The University of Minnesota opened its doors in 1851, and in 1868 purchased land southeast of the city to establish an agricultural school and farm. But the first year a program was offered, no students enrolled. Undeterred, the administration maintained its commitment to the teaching of farming, and in 1894 the school offered the first U.S. ag-school course in dressing and curing meat. Today, the Minnesota Beef Expo in St. Paul draws thousands of visitors to its exhibits and judging events and the state carries on its proud tradition of raising championship cattle. This recipe, featuring state-raised beef, won first place at a recent Minnesota beef cook-off.

PEPPERY PEACH SALSA

- 1   small red bell pepper, seeded and coarsely chopped
- ½   cup peach preserves
- ¼   cup sliced green onions, including 1 inch green parts
- 2   tablespoons diced canned jalapeño chilies, drained
- 1   tablespoon fresh lemon juice
- 1   clove garlic, minced
- ¼   teaspoon ground ginger
- ⅛   teaspoon salt

- 1½   pounds 1-inch-thick boneless beef top loin steak, cut into 4 pieces
- ¼   teaspoon salt
- ¼   teaspoon freshly ground black pepper
- 1   red bell pepper, seeded and cut into rings

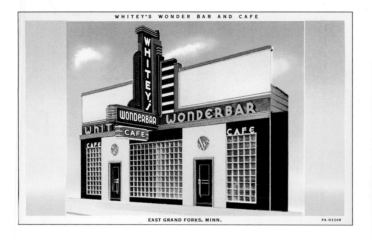

WHITEY'S WONDER BAR AND CAFE

EAST GRAND FORKS, MINN.   8A-H2206

Build a low fire in a charcoal grill or heat a gas grill to 325°F.

To make the peach salsa: Combine all the ingredients in a small nonreactive bowl and gently stir until blended. Reserve 2 tablespoons of the salsa to brush on the steak as it cooks. Set the rest aside.

Season the steak pieces on both sides by rubbing them with the salt and pepper. Oil the grill grate, add the steak pieces, cover the grill, and cook, turning once, for 8 to 9 minutes per side for medium-rare, 10 to 12 minutes per side for medium. (They will lose flavor if you cook them to well done.) During the last few minutes of cooking, lightly brush the top of the steaks with the reserved 2 tablespoons salsa, turn, brush again, and cook just until the topping is sizzling. To serve, top each piece with a red pepper ring and fill each ring with some of the remaining salsa.

Serves 4

DETROIT LAKES MINNESOTA

Greetings from
MISSISSIPPI

Catfish with Tomato–Black Bean Relish

In *Life on the Mississippi,* Mark Twain tells the lively tale of Jacques Marquette's encounter with a two-hundred-pound catfish. "Big cats" have been sighted in the Mississippi since the mid-nineteenth century, although today's sportfishermen seek giants closer to one hundred pounds. Today, the catfish most of us put on our plates comes from fish farms, free of the muddy taste often associated with wild fish. Mississippi leads the world in the production of pond-raised catfish, and Humphreys County, with more than thirty thousand acres of ponds, is the Catfish Capital of the World. The annual World Catfish Festival held every April in Belzoni serves up plenty of catfish. Look for catfish in your supermarket. Although they're mild flavored, they hold up well to grilling, and marry nicely with spicy relishes and sauces. Serve this dish with corn bread and a green salad.

TOMATO–BLACK BEAN RELISH

2   tablespoons olive oil
1   small onion, chopped
2   stalks celery, chopped
3   cloves garlic, minced
3   jalapeño chilies, seeded and minced
1   can (15 ounces) black beans, rinsed and drained

1   can (14.5 ounces) diced tomatoes
1   cup fresh or frozen corn kernels
Juice of ½ lemon (about 2 tablespoons)
Salt and freshly ground black pepper to taste

4   catfish fillets (4 to 6 ounces each)
½   teaspoon garlic salt
Freshly ground black pepper to taste

To make the black bean relish: Heat the olive oil in a medium nonreactive saucepan over medium-low heat. Add the onion, celery, garlic, and jalapeños and sauté for 5 minutes, or until the onions are translucent. Add the beans, tomatoes and their juice, and corn and simmer over low heat, stirring occasionally, for 30 minutes, or until the salsa is thickened. Stir in the lemon juice and salt and pepper. Set aside.

Build a medium-hot fire in a charcoal grill or heat a gas grill to 375°F. Sprinkle the catfish fillets with the garlic salt and pepper on both sides and place them in a well-oiled grill basket or directly on a well-oiled grill. Cook for 5 minutes per side, or until the fish flakes easily with a fork. Serve topped with a spoonful of relish.

Serves 4

Kansas City Ribs

Ribs change their stripes, and their flavors, from one state to another. In Kansas City, they're juicy and spicy and served everywhere. Recipes for them are a closely guarded secret at the American Royal Cookoff, held each October, which attracts thousands of visitors. True Kansas City barbecued ribs are slowly cooked in a smoker. This recipe for grilled ribs can be cooked in any simple backyard gas or charcoal grill, but they're flavored by smoke that comes from tossing wood chunks on the fire. (Look for these at your local hardware store or any place that sells barbecue grills.) Do read all the way through the recipe before you begin, and be sure to follow all the steps. The results will be worth it. The Rib Rub imparts a wonderful flavor, and the Mop Sauce keeps the ribs moist without burning. If you're new to cooking a slab of ribs, be sure to measure the width of your grill before you go shopping to ensure that you come home with meat that will fit with the cover closed. Serve with Coleslaw (page 116) and Corn Muffins (page 121).

4-pound slab pork ribs

RIB RUB

1	teaspoon salt
1	teaspoon chili powder
½	teaspoon freshly ground black pepper
½	teaspoon dry mustard
½	teaspoon Hungarian paprika
¼	teaspoon cayenne pepper
¼	teaspoon onion powder
⅛	teaspoon garlic powder

MOP SAUCE

1	cup beef broth
½	cup vegetable oil
1	tablespoon Worcestershire sauce
1	tablespoon vinegar (any kind)
½	teaspoon molasses
¼	teaspoon hot sauce

4	cups wood chunks (preferably apple and hickory)
3	to 4 cups apple juice or water

Barbecue sauce for serving (optional)

The night before grilling, place the slab of ribs on a sheet of aluminum foil a little more than twice the length of the slab. Dry the ribs with paper towels.

To make the rib rub: Combine all the ingredients in a small bowl and stir with a fork until blended. Apply the rub to both sides of the ribs. Cover the ribs with the foil and refrigerate for 8 to 24 hours. (The longer you leave the rub on before cooking, the more the flavors will permeate the meat.)

To make the mop sauce: Combine all the ingredients in a glass jar with a tight-fitting lid and shake until well blended.

Soak the wood chunks in water for 30 minutes. Build a medium indirect fire in a charcoal grill using a drip pan or heat a gas grill to 350°F and prepare it for indirect heat using a drip pan (see page 11). Fill the drip pan half full with apple juice. Drain a handful of wood chunks and place on the coals, or place all the chunks in a perforated foil packet and add to the gas grill (see page 9). Place the ribs on the grate over the drip pan. Cover the grill and cook for 20 minutes. Turn the ribs and baste with the mop sauce. Continue to cook, covered, turning the ribs and basting them with sauce every 20 minutes or so. For a charcoal grill, add more drained wood chunks each time you turn the ribs, and add more charcoal after 30 to 45 minutes. Cook for 75 to 90 minutes, or until the ribs are dark brown and aromatic. (To test for doneness, slice off one end rib and sample it.)

Transfer the ribs to a carving board, cover loosely with aluminum foil, and let rest for at least 5 minutes. Slice between the bones with a sharp knife to divide.

Serve with your favorite barbecue sauce, if you wish.

Serves 4 to 6

Grilled Walleye

With their long, tapering bodies and silvery skins, walleyes are prized catches in Montana's lakes and rivers. As many as 35 million are stocked in state waters each year. Groups such as Walleyes Unlimited work hard to improve water quality and habitats, and to protect spawning grounds. Boys and girls who attend Camp Walleye have a chance to try their luck and get tips from some of the state's best fishermen. Throughout the summer, anglers vie for cash prizes in numerous tournaments, including five events in the Montana Walleye Circuit. To date, the biggest walleye caught in the state weighed 16 pounds, 10 ounces. Members of the perch family, walleyes have lean, delicately flavored white flesh and relatively few bones. They taste delicious grilled, but care must be taken to prevent over-cooking them. Serve with Mom's Potato Salad (page 117). If you don't have a fisherman in the family, substitute ocean perch or tilapia fillets.

4   **walleye fillets (6 to 8 ounces each)**

4   **tablespoons butter, plus more for greasing foil**

2   **teaspoons Hungarian paprika**

2   **teaspoons lemon pepper**

Salt to taste

Build a medium fire in a charcoal grill or heat a gas grill to 350°F. Spread 2 pieces of aluminum foil out on the counter, each large enough to accommodate 2 fillets lengthwise. Grease the foil with butter. Place 2 fillets on each piece of foil. Leaving the foil flat (don't wrap up the fish), crimp the edges slightly to keep any juices from draining off. Melt the butter in a small saucepan over low heat. Add the paprika, lemon pepper, and salt and stir with a whisk until smooth. Brush the fillets on both sides with the butter mixture.

Carefully place the fish on their foil trays on the grill. Cover and cook for 5 to 8 minutes, or until the fish flakes easily and is opaque throughout. Slide a spatula under each fillet and transfer it to a dinner plate.

Serves 4

Grilled Pot Roast Pipérade

Omaha celebrated its position as the eastern terminus for America's first transcontinental railroad with a groundbreaking celebration in 1863. Eight years later, its first meatpacking plant opened. Before the decade ended, meat from cattle raised and fattened on the plains of Nebraska was being packed and shipped to hundreds of destinations, including England. The state currently boasts that it is home to more cows than people—a 4 to 1 ratio—and it produces more than 20 percent of the country's beef. Beef chuck, an inexpensive cut of meat that requires long, slow cooking, is popular throughout the state, emblematic of common sense and good value. Here's a clever way to prepare it on the grill, and make a fine Sunday dinner without heating up the kitchen. You will need a large aluminum foil cooking bag for this recipe, or see the note at the end.

1 tablespoon all-purpose flour

2 tablespoons minced garlic

1 tablespoon coarsely ground black peppercorns

1 boneless beef chuck shoulder pot roast (about 2½ pounds)

1 onion, cut into 8 wedges

1 red bell pepper, seeded and cut into 2-inch-wide strips

1 yellow bell pepper, seeded and cut into 2-inch-wide strips

½ cup beef broth

2 tablespoons thinly sliced fresh basil

Salt and freshly ground black pepper to taste

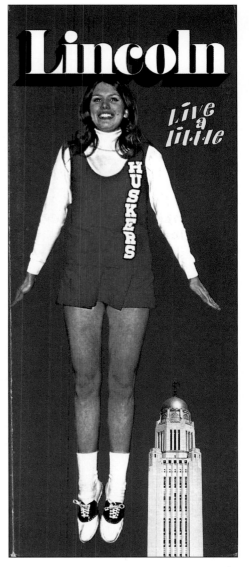

Sprinkle the inside of a large aluminum foil cooking bag with the flour. Combine the garlic and peppercorns in a small bowl and press them into all surfaces of the pot roast. Place the pot roast in the cooking bag. Add the onion wedges and bell pepper strips and pour in the beef broth. Seal the bag by double-folding the open end.

Build a medium indirect fire in a charcoal grill using a drip pan or heat a gas grill to 350°F and prepare it for indirect heat using a drip pan (see page 11). Place the pot roast in its bag directly on the grate over the drip pan, cover, and cook for 2 to 2½ hours, adding more coals every 45 minutes to maintain even heat, until the pot roast is fork-tender. Using oven mitts, transfer the pouch from the grill to a sturdy platter. Carefully cut and fold back the top of the bag, allowing the steam to escape. Using a long-handled fork, transfer the vegetables to a serving bowl, toss with the basil, and cover to keep warm. Transfer the pot roast to a cutting board and carve into slices. Season the beef and vegetables with salt and pepper and serve immediately.

Serves 6

Note: If you don't have a cooking bag, make an aluminum foil pouch. Place a 28-by-18-inch sheet of heavy-duty aluminum foil in a shallow roasting pan. Sprinkle the foil with the flour. Place the seasoned pot roast in the center of the foil. Add the onion, bell pepper, and beef broth. Bring the two long sides of the foil up over the pot roast and seal loosely with a double fold. Fold in the open ends to seal. If necessary, wrap with a second piece of foil going the other way, to keep the roast completely covered.

Prime Rib

Las Vegas, the Silver State's gambling paradise, has long been the land of prime rib. This flavorful cut of meat shows up on hundreds of menus all across the city, with the largest cut, the Diamond Jim Brady, weighing 28 to 32 ounces. Restaurants are fiercely proud of offering special deals, which range from under-$12 early-bird specials to slices carved from a roast right at your table. You'll need to win big to pay for dinner at the city's fanciest restaurants, so it's much more economical to cook your own prime rib, which becomes a juicy and flavorful treat when grilled. Serve with Roasted Corn (page 36) and Barbecued Sweet Potatoes (page 78). Leftovers make fabulous sandwiches.

1   standing beef rib roast
      (6 to 8 pounds)
Salt and freshly ground
      black pepper to taste

Build a low indirect fire in a charcoal grill using a drip pan or heat a gas grill to 325°F and prepare it for indirect heat using a drip pan (see page 11). Rub the rib roast all over with salt and pepper. Oil the grill grate and add the roast over indirect heat. Cover the grill, open the lid vents halfway, and cook for 1½ to 2 hours, adding more charcoal every 30 to 45 minutes as necessary and allowing 14 minutes per pound cooking time. Check the roast for doneness with an instant-read thermometer. Remove it from the grill at 120°F for rare, 130°F for medium-rare, or 140°F for medium. Cover the roast loosely with aluminum foil and let it rest for 30 minutes before carving. The temperature will rise by as much as 10°F as it rests.

Serves 10 to 12

Note: You don't need to rob a bank to buy a prime rib. Ask the butcher at your local supermarket to find out when it goes on sale and buy it at $4.99 a pound or better. Many supermarkets carry limited quantities and don't advertise lower prices.

Granite State Venison with Currant Sauce

The whitetail deer is New Hampshire's state animal. While trophy bucks are getting harder to find as more houses go up, each year a few Granite Staters bring home deer that weigh more than two hundred pounds. Hunters seeking venison frequent the central and southern portions of the state, where the deer densities are the highest, while those looking for the adventure of a deep-woods hunting experience find better conditions in the White Mountains and the most northern sections. For those who prefer to buy meat, a number of online businesses sell venison. This recipe uses tender pieces cut from the loin, which can also be cooked in a grill pan.

2   tablespoons olive oil

¼   cup orange juice

1   tablespoon fresh thyme leaves, or 1 teaspoon dried thyme

¼   teaspoon freshly ground black pepper

4   venison medallions (about 4 ounces each)

CURRANT SAUCE

½   cup dry red wine

½   cup fresh orange juice

3   tablespoons red currant jelly

½   cup pitted and chopped prunes

The night before cooking, combine the olive oil, orange juice, thyme, and pepper in a shallow nonreactive roasting pan and stir with a whisk to blend. Add the venison medallions and turn once. Cover with plastic wrap and refrigerate overnight.

Build a medium-hot fire in a charcoal grill or heat a gas grill to 375°F.

To make the currant sauce: Combine the wine and orange juice in a medium nonreactive saucepan and bring to a boil over medium-hot heat. Add the currant jelly and stir with a whisk until smooth. Reduce the heat to medium-low and cook, stirring occasionally, for 10 minutes, or until the sauce is slightly reduced. Add the prunes, reduce the heat to low, and cook, stirring occasionally, for 10 minutes, or until the sauce is thickened and the prunes are integrated into the sauce. Set sauce aside.

Oil the grill grate. Using tongs, transfer the medallions to the grill. Discard the marinade. Cook the medallions for 2 to 3 minutes on each side, using the tongs to turn. Transfer to a platter, cover loosely with aluminum foil, and let rest for 10 minutes. Serve with a spoonful of the currant sauce.

Serves 4

Greetings from NEW JERSEY

Jersey Dogs

Beloved ballpark and cookout fare and one of America's first fast foods, hot hogs have been part of our culinary history for more than one hundred years. In 1939, Eleanor Roosevelt and Pres. Franklin D. Roosevelt presided over a picnic honoring King George VI where hot dogs were prominently featured. While it might seem like a no-brainer to simply toss a few on the grill for the kids, hot dog cookery is still taken seriously in New Jersey, especially in the northern section of the state. At least two purveyors—Syd's in Union and Jerry's in Elizabeth—serve big dogs, first simmered in water and then charbroiled. Try this technique on your grill to enjoy a real Jersey dog. Look for all-beef brands that come four or five to a pound. If you can't find them in your local super-market, order them online from www.windmillfastfoods.com.

1   teaspoon celery salt
6   Jersey hot dogs
6   hot dog buns
Mustard, ketchup, and relish
    for serving

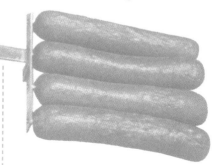

Build a medium fire in a charcoal grill or heat a gas grill to 350°F. Bring a large pot of water to a boil over high heat, reduce the heat to low, add the celery salt and hot dogs, and simmer for at least 15 minutes, or until the grill is ready.

Oil the grill grate. Drain the hot dogs and put them on the grill while they're still hot. Using tongs, turn them every 30 seconds until they're nicely browned, cooking them for a total of about 4 minutes. Serve immediately in the buns, with mustard, ketchup, and relish.

Serves 6

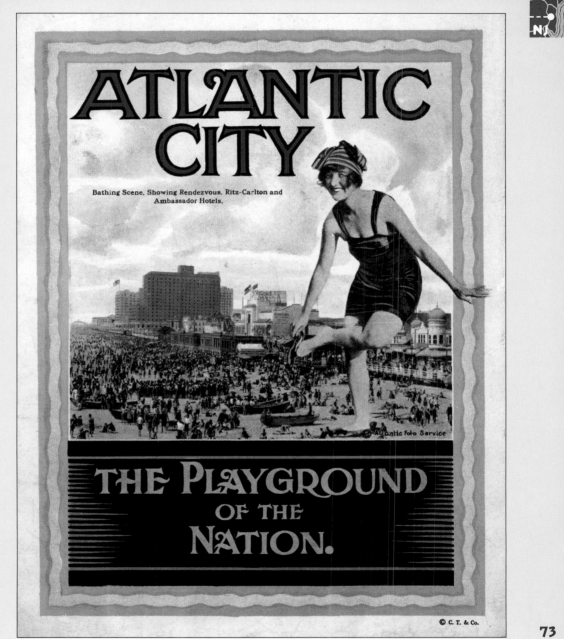

ATLANTIC CITY

Bathing Scene, Showing Rendezvous, Ritz-Carlton and Ambassador Hotels.

© Atlantic Foto Service

THE PLAYGROUND
OF THE
NATION.

© C. T. & Co.

Greetings from New Mexico

Land of Enchantment

Grilled Green Chili—Stuffed Pepper Steaks

The Southwest is prized for its spicy, hot flavors and intermingling of culinary traditions from Native American, Mexican, and Spanish cooking. One of the region's culinary stars is the Anaheim, or New Mexican, pepper, which has been grown commercially since the 1900s. This moderately hot chili is sold either light green, dark green, or red, ranging from 6 to 10 inches long. It's also the chili used for decorative *ristras,* strings of dried red chilies.

Tucked inside these pepper-crusted steaks, roasted chilies are a delightful surprise. Substitute filet mignon or sirloin steaks for the rib eyes, and if you're not a fan of black pepper, omit the peppercorns and use pepper bacon instead. You can also use roasted jalapeño chilies instead of Anaheims. Thinly slice leftover steak and put it on sourdough bread with Muenster cheese and more roasted chilies for a Southwestern steak sandwich.

4	boneless rib eye steaks, 1 to 2 inches thick
4	New Mexican (Anaheim) chilies, roasted and peeled (see note)
4	strips bacon (optional)
2	tablespoons black peppercorns
2	tablespoons hot sauce, preferably Cuban habanero
2	tablespoons Worcestershire sauce
2	tablespoons soy sauce
2	tablespoons rice vinegar
½	teaspoon garlic powder

Two hours before grilling, with a sharp knife, slice a horizontal pocket in the side of each steak, being careful not to cut all the way through the edges. Place a roasted chili in each pocket. (Wrap a strip of bacon, if using, around each steak horizontally and secure with a toothpick.) Place the peppercorns in a sturdy paper bag and pound with a hammer, or grind in a mortar, until coarsely crushed. Pour the crushed pepper onto a plate and press each steak into them to coat both sides. Combine the hot sauce, Worcestershire sauce, soy sauce, vinegar, and garlic in a shallow, nonreactive dish and whisk until blended.

A PICTURESQUE HOME OF THE SOUTHWEST

Recreational Map of **NEW MEXICO** **LAND OF ENCHANTMENT**

Add the steaks, turn to cover with the marinade, cover with plastic wrap, and refrigerate for 2 hours. Remove from the refrigerator 30 minutes before cooking.

Build a medium fire in a charcoal grill or heat a gas grill to 350°F. Oil the grill grate, add the steaks, and cook, turning every 3 minutes, for a total of 12 minutes, or until an instant-read thermometer reaches 150°F for medium-rare.

Serve immediately with a green salad and sliced tomatoes.

Serves 4

Note: To roast the peppers, place them under a hot broiler, or grill them, turning every 2 minutes, until the skins are blackened. Put them in a paper bag, close the bag, and let cool for 15 minutes. Rub off the blackened skin with your finger and remove the seeds.

Spiedies

Popular in central New York's Broome County, these marinated morsels are extremely versatile and great fun to grill. Culinary legend says they originated with Italian immigrants who came to Binghamton in the late 1920s. The first spiedies were made with lamb, and the name derives from the Italian word *spiedini,* for kabobs. While some spiedie fans insist that the meat must be threaded on skewers, many participants at Binghamton's Annual Spiedie Cooking Contest, held in early August, spoon the cubes directly onto the grate and turn them several times with a spatula until they're done. Just about every kind of meat has been featured at this event, including moose and venison. Experiment with seasonings, using dried mint for lamb, rosemary for pork, red wine for beef. Allow the meat to marinate for 24 to 48 hours. Make an extra batch of marinade to use as a sauce for the cooked spiedies, or search online for authentic bottled spiedie sauce (www.brooksbbq.com and www.spiedies.com are two sources). And be vigilant with the cooking and turning. The meat cooks in a jiffy after its long bath in the marinade. For a cookout party, grill several different kinds of spiedies and serve on submarine sandwich rolls, split French bread, or atop a bed of lettuce, drizzled with extra sauce or your favorite Italian dressing. Note: Never, ever use ketchup or other condiments. Leftover cold spiedies taste great in sandwiches, too.

½	cup olive oil
½	cup dry white wine
¼	cup vinegar (any kind)
4	cloves garlic, crushed and minced
1	teaspoon salt
¼	teaspoon freshly ground black pepper
1	teaspoon dried oregano
1	teaspoon dried thyme
4	pounds boneless chicken, beef, pork, or lamb, cut into 1½-inch cubes (big enough so they won't slip through your grill's grate)

MOST UNIQUE TERRACE BETWEEN NEW YORK & BUFFALO

One to 2 days before grilling, combine all the ingredients except the meat in a large nonreactive bowl and whisk until smooth. Add the meat and toss until well coated with the marinade. Cover tightly with plastic wrap and refrigerate for 24 to 48 hours, stirring several times to be sure the meat is evenly coated with marinade. (Or, combine all ingredients in a heavy-duty resealable plastic bag, seal, and shake. Add the meat, seal again, and store flat in the refrigerator. Turn once or twice during the marinating time.)

Build a medium fire in a charcoal grill or heat a gas grill to 350°F. Oil the grill grate. Using a slotted spoon, remove the spiedies from the marinade, place them on the grill in batches, and cook, turning with a spatula every 3 or 4 minutes, for a total of 10 to 12 minutes, or until they are done to suit your taste. (Sample a few, being careful not to overcook.) Using tongs, transfer the cooked spiedies to a serving platter. Discard the marinade. Serve hot or warm.

Serves 10 to 12

Barbecued Sweet Potatoes

Roasted in the coals of an evening fire, ash-baked sweet potatoes were an old-time Southern delicacy. Today, North Carolina hosts sweet potato festivals in September and October, and honors the sweet potato as its official state vegetable. The state annually harvests approximately 550 million pounds of the bright-orange-fleshed varieties 'Beauregard,' 'Hernandez,' and 'Jewel,' which make up about 40 percent of the nation's crop. Cultivated in the South as early as the mid-seventeenth century, this native American food contains more fiber than oatmeal and is high in vitamins A and C, making it a healthful alternative to white potatoes. Sweet potatoes taste great when grilled. Plan ahead and soak them in this piquant marinade to complement their sweet flavor. Serve with ham, roast beef, steaks, or chicken.

SPICY MARINADE

- ½   **cup cider vinegar**
- 2   **tablespoons olive oil**
- 2   **tablespoons packed brown sugar**
- 1   **teaspoon salt**
- 2   **teaspoons red pepper flakes**
- 1   **teaspoon cayenne pepper**
- ½   **teaspoon freshly ground black pepper**

- 4   **sweet potatoes**

Three to 4 hours before grilling, make the spicy marinade: Combine all the ingredients in a nonreactive bowl and blend with a whisk until smooth. Peel the sweet potatoes, cut them in half lengthwise, and cut each half into 2 crosswise pieces. You will have large chunks 2½ to 3 inches long. Add the sweet potato chunks to the marinade and turn to coat. Cover with plastic wrap and marinate at room temperature for 3 to 4 hours, turning the pieces several times.

Build a medium fire in a charcoal grill or heat a gas grill to 350°F. Oil the grill grate. Using tongs, place the sweet potato chunks on the grill and cook, turning every few minutes, for 10 to 15 minutes, or until the sweet potatoes are fork-tender and lightly browned on the outside. Serve hot.

Serves 4 to 6

OPPORTUNITIES
AGRICULTURAL
BUNCOMBE COUNTY
"Land of the Sky"

OPPORTUNITIES
INDUSTRIAL
ASHEVILLE. N. C.
"Land of the Sky"

IN THE
HEART OF
THE BLUE
RIDGE

STOCK RAISING
DAIRY PRODUCTS
TRUCK FARMING
FRUIT & GRAIN
GROWING
GOOD MARKETS
GOOD ROADS

ISSUED BY ASHEVILLE BOARD OF TRADE, ASHEVILLE, N.C.

Sirloin Ribbons

In 1883, when he was twenty-five years old, Theodore Roosevelt joined a hunting party in the Dakota Territory, and was so taken with the majestic country that he eventually established two sizable cattle ranches there. The vast grasslands proved the perfect site to fatten cattle for the Chicago market. Today, beef cattle production is the state's number-one livestock industry, and farms, ranches, cropland, and pastures occupy 90 percent of the land. Theodore Roosevelt National Park honors America's early conservationist, and it also provides charcoal grates at each park campsite. Try this recipe there, or in your own backyard. Since the meat is very thinly sliced, it cooks quickly. Leftovers make great steak sandwiches. Serve with sliced cucumbers and Grilled Tomato–Bread Salad (page 82).

2	pounds beef sirloin steak
3	tablespoons fresh lemon juice
3	tablespoons soy sauce
1	teaspoon hot sauce (optional)

Two hours before grilling, slice the sirloin into ¼-inch-thick strips with a sharp knife. In a nonreactive baking dish, combine the lemon juice, soy sauce, and hot sauce, if using. Stir with a whisk until blended. Lay the steak strips in the marinade and turn with a fork until all sides are coated. Cover with plastic wrap and refrigerate for 2 hours, turning several more times.

Soak 6 long wooden skewers in water to cover for 30 minutes. Build a medium fire in a charcoal grill or heat a gas grill to 350°F.

Remove the beef from the marinade and thread onto the skewers, letting the meat take an S shape as it is pierced by the skewer. Discard

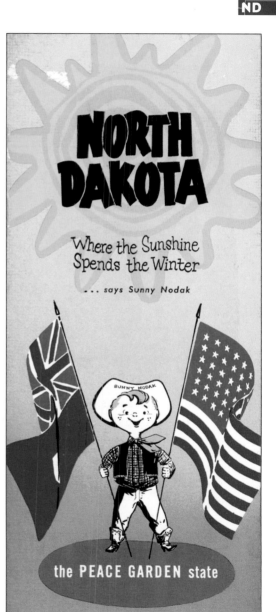

the marinade. Oil the grill grate, add the skewers, and cook for 2 minutes on each side, or until the meat is browned and sizzling. Serve immediately.

Serves 4 to 6

Grilled Tomato–Bread Salad

In 1870, Ohio seedsman Alexander Livingston introduced a tomato called 'Paragon,' a smooth-skinned, uniform-size round variety that was remarkably unlike the bumpy, hollow-cavity tomatoes of the time. He went on to produce more than thirty other tomato varieties between 1870 and 1941, putting Ohio on the map as the birthplace of the commercial tomato. His work also inspired the town fathers of Reynoldsburg, Livingston's birthplace, to host the annual Tomato Festival, which offers prizes for the tallest tomato plant and the largest tomato. Today, Ohio ranks third in tomato production for the country, and tomato juice is the state's official beverage.

When you have a few too many ripe tomatoes on your kitchen counter, make this succulent salad, which tastes best prepared a day in advance. You can make this salad without grilling either the bread or the tomatoes, but fire brings out special flavors in both ingredients. Since the bread and the tomatoes cook quickly, grill them after you've cooked another meal, to make use of the hot coals, and assemble the salad in the evening to enjoy the next day. Serve with an omelet or sliced ham and a green salad.

4	slices Italian or country bread, about ½ inch thick
½	cup olive oil
6	tomatoes, cut into ¼-inch-thick slices
2	tablespoons white balsamic vinegar
2	cloves garlic, minced
1	tablespoon Dijon mustard
2	tablespoons chopped fresh basil
	Salt and freshly ground black pepper to taste

Build a medium fire in a charcoal grill or heat a gas grill to 350°F. Brush the bread on both sides with some of the olive oil and toast on the edges of a well-oiled grate for about 30 seconds on each side, turning with tongs and watching constantly to keep it from burning. Set aside. Brush the tomatoes with a bit more of the olive oil and cook on the grate, turning them with a spatula, for about 3 minutes on each side, or until they begin to shrivel. Scoop them into a bowl.

Combine the remaining olive oil, vinegar, garlic, mustard, and basil in a medium nonreactive bowl. Blend with a whisk until smooth. Cut the bread into ½-inch dice. Cut the tomato slices into smaller pieces and add them to the dressing along with any juices that have accumulated in the bowl. Toss well. Let the mixture sit at room temperature for about 1 hour. Toss again and season with salt and pepper. Cover with plastic wrap and refrigerate overnight. Remove from the refrigerator, season again to taste with salt and pepper, and let the mixture stand at room temperature for about 3 hours before serving.

Serves 4 to 6

Marinated Flank Steak with Grilled Peppers

In the mid-1860s, drovers brought cattle from Texas north along the Chisholm Trail, stopping in Oklahoma to fatten their herds on the lush prairie grasses. The National Cowboy and Western Heritage Museum in Oklahoma City tells the story of these rugged workers, and to keep their legacy alive, towns throughout the state offer chuck wagon cook-offs, stays at guest ranches, and plenty of trail rides. (Oklahoma claims to be home to more horses than any other state.) Cattle remains the state's largest agricultural industry, and farmers are proud of the numerous breeds they raise, including the mighty Texas Longhorn. The lean, boneless flank steak, which benefits from marinating, is a good choice for quick and tasty grilling. Serve it with Ranch Beans (page 119) and Coleslaw (page 116).

SOY MARINADE

- ¼ cup dry red wine, preferably Zinfandel
- ¼ cup soy sauce
- 2 tablespoons olive oil
- 1 tablespoon white balsamic vinegar
- 1 tablespoon packed brown sugar
- 2 cloves garlic, minced

- 1 beef flank steak (about 2 pounds)
- 3 large red bell peppers, seeded and cut into 2-inch-wide strips
- ¼ cup olive oil

OK

The night before grilling, make the soy marinade: Combine all the ingredients in a nonreactive baking dish and stir with a whisk until smooth. Add the flank steak, cover with plastic wrap, and refrigerate for 8 hours or overnight, turning once. Remove the steak from the refrigerator 30 minutes before cooking.

Build a medium fire in a charcoal grill or heat a gas grill to 350°F. Oil the grill grate. Using tongs, remove the steak from the marinade and place it on the grate. Toss the bell pepper strips with the olive oil in a nonreactive bowl and, using tongs, place them on the grate. Cook the steak for 8 minutes per side for medium-rare. Cook the peppers for about 4 minutes per side, or until they are soft, sizzling, and slightly browned on the edges. Cut the steak into slices against the grain and serve with 3 or 4 pepper strips.

Serves 4

Sirloin steak

Round steak
Needs tendering

Flank steak
Needs tendering

Backyard Peach Melba

In 1847, Henderson Luelling set out to travel from Iowa to Oregon along the Oregon Trail. In his wagon, he carried his wife, eight children, and some seven hundred young fruit trees, including 'Early Crawford,' 'Late Crawford,' and 'Golden Cling' peach trees. The nursery he established in 1848 near Milwaukie supplied fledgling home orchards throughout the Oregon Territory. He expanded his stock in time to benefit from the end of the state's gold rush and the beginning of Oregon's fruit industry. Today, the newer 'Oregold' peach is one of the tastiest varieties on earth, a premium fruit sold by Medford's seventy-five-year-old gourmet fruit company, Harry & David. Buy juicy, ripe peaches for this delicious dessert.

RASPBERRY SAUCE

½   cup seedless raspberry jam

½   cup dry red wine

2   tablespoons fresh lemon juice

8   large, ripe peaches

1   pint vanilla ice cream

Soak 16 long wooden skewers in water for 30 minutes. Build a medium fire in a charcoal grill or heat a gas grill to 350°F.

To make the raspberry sauce: Combine all the ingredients in a small, heavy, nonreactive saucepan and cook over medium heat, stirring frequently, for 10 minutes, until the mixture bubbles and begins to thicken slightly. Keep the sauce warm over low heat or carry it to the grill and reheat it over the fire as you cook the peaches.

Cut the peaches in half and use a teaspoon to gently remove the pits, keeping the halves intact. Thread 2 peach halves onto 2 parallel skewers, running the skewers just to the right and left sides of the center of each half and

keeping the cut sides facing the same way.
(The parallel skewering will keep the peach
halves from twirling around when you turn
them over.) Repeat until all the peaches are
threaded. Lay the skewers on a large platter,
with all the peaches cut side down.

Oil the grill grate. Lay the peaches, cut side up,
on the grill grate and cook for 4 minutes, or
until the skins begin to brown and slight grill
marks appear. Brush the tops with the raspberry
sauce and turn the peaches over. Cook for 3
minutes, or until the sauce sizzles. Slide the
peaches off the grate, turn onto serving plates,
cut side up, and top each half with a scoop of
vanilla ice cream. Spoon additional warm sauce
on top.

Serves 4

South Philly Hamburgers

The hamburger is the hands-down favorite All-American sandwich. Beginning with National Burger Month in May, every summer we eat millions of them at cookouts. Most of us slather them with ketchup, mustard, and/or relish, and fill the buns with cheese, lettuce, onions, and other fixings. Every state has its hamburger legends. In Pennsylvania, where Henry Heinz started selling ketchup in 1875, the state's very first motel, built in 1936 near State College, served hamburgers for 8 cents, cheeseburgers for 10 cents. And today, a pub in Clearfield offers its own famous whopper—a six-pound burger that sells for $23.95 and comes with a prize for any customer who can eat it in three hours. The South Philly burger, which originated with Philadelphia's Italian immigrant cooks, is enhanced with flavorings that make it moist and reminiscent of meat loaf.

1½   pounds ground beef chuck

1   egg

1   small onion, minced

1   large clove garlic, minced

2   teaspoons dried basil

2   teaspoons dried oregano

¼   teaspoon salt

¼   teaspoon freshly ground black pepper

6   slices provolone cheese

6   hamburger buns, split

Ketchup, mustard, and relish for serving

Combine the meat, egg, onion, garlic, basil, oregano, salt, and pepper in a medium bowl. With clean hands, mix lightly until the ingredients are combined. Shape the mixture into 6 patties. (The mixture can be refrigerated for up to 6 hours before cooking.)

Build a medium fire in a charcoal grill or heat a gas grill to 350°F. Oil the grill grate, add the patties, and cook for 5 to 7 minutes per side, or until they are no longer pink inside and register 160°F on an instant-read thermometer. Move the burgers to the cool edges of the grill and place a slice of cheese on top of each burger. Put the buns, split side down, near the burgers on the edge of the grill. Cover the grill and cook for 1 minute. Assemble the burgers and serve immediately.

Serves 6

Grilled Pizzas

From 1898 to 1932, steamships brought a large number of southern Italian immigrants to Rhode Island. Today, Italian-American communities flourish in the Providence neighborhoods of Federal Hill, Silver Lake, and the North End, as well as in other cities throughout the state. For decades, family-owned and -operated pizza places have served memorable pies. In 1980, when Johanne Killeen and George Germon opened Al Forno on Steeple Street in Providence, they put in a wood-burning grill and served up grilled pizza. Its hauntingly delicious crisp crust inspired many local cooks to experiment with making pizza over an open fire. The recipe below uses premade dough from the grocery store or pizza parlor. Add your favorite toppings: grilled vegetables, other cheeses, or even thin slices of barbecued meat or chicken.

1	pound refrigerated pizza dough
¼	cup olive oil
½	cup tomato sauce
½	cup (2 ounces) shredded mozzarella or Swiss cheese
6	to 8 fresh basil leaves, thinly sliced

Three to 4 hours before grilling, remove the chilled packaged dough from the refrigerator. (If you use chilled dough, it won't stretch enough.)

Build a medium indirect fire with the coals on one side in a charcoal grill or heat a gas grill to 350°F and prepare it for indirect heat (see page 11).

Cut the room-temperature dough into 4 equal pieces. Spread one piece of dough out on a greased baking sheet and stretch and flatten with your hands to make a round or rectangle about ⅛ inch thick and 6 to 8 inches wide or long. The dough will spring back several times. You can also hold it up in front of you like a

pizza shop pro and gently stretch it out. Don't worry about making a perfect round or rectangle, and do not create a raised outer crust. Try to get it as thin as you can.

Oil the grill grate. Drape the dough on the grate over the hot part of the grill, stretching it as you put it down to keep it as thin as possible. Watch it closely. As soon as it begins to bubble, in about 1 minute, grab one end with tongs, drag it over onto the cool part of the grill, and flip it over. Immediately brush the top with some of the olive oil, spread on about 2 tablespoons of the tomato sauce,

and scatter one-fourth of the cheese on top. Grab one side of the pizza with the tongs and gently slide it back over the hot part of the grill. Cook for about 30 seconds. With the tongs, move the pizza back to the cool part of the grill, cover the grill, and cook for 1 minute, or until

the cheese is melted. Scatter a bit of the basil on top, lift the pizza off the grate with a metal spatula, and serve immediately. Repeat to make the other 3 pizzas.

Makes 4 small pizzas; serves 2 to 4

Greetings from SOUTH CAROLINA

Grilled Tuna with Mustard Sauce

I n 1931, the city of Charleston established the Old and Historic District, and in the decades since, local groups have worked hard to preserve much of the eighteenth- and nineteenth-century architecture, making the city a great place to explore on foot. If you visit Charleston and go out for dinner at one of the fabulous local seafood restaurants, chances are you'll find grilled tuna on the menu. The city offers world-class offshore saltwater fishing, and its harbor buzzes with the activity of sportfish charters and numerous tournaments. The biggest yellowfin tuna caught to date in South Carolina weighed 241 pounds, but local fishermen win prizes for 50-pound catches as well. This recipe combines tuna with mustard, another popular grilling sauce ingredient in some parts of the state. Serve with white rice and a cucumber salad.

Build a medium fire in a charcoal grill or heat a gas grill to 350°F.

To make the mustard sauce: Combine the mustard, vinegar, honey, and wine in a small nonreactive saucepan and stir with a whisk until smooth. Bring to a boil over medium-hot heat, reduce the heat to low, and simmer for 5 minutes. Stir in the capers and yogurt, season with salt and pepper, and remove from the heat.

Oil the grill grate. Brush the tops of the tuna steaks with olive oil and place the steaks on the grill, oiled side down. Brush the tops of the steaks with olive oil. Cook for 5 minutes on each side, or until they flake easily with a fork. Serve topped with a spoonful of mustard sauce.

MUSTARD SAUCE

¼ cup whole-grain Dijon mustard
¼ cup cider vinegar
1 tablespoon honey
¼ cup dry white wine
1 tablespoon capers, drained
¼ cup plain yogurt
Salt and freshly ground black pepper to taste

4 tuna steaks (4 ounces each)
Olive oil for brushing

Serves 4

Myrtle Beach
SOUTH CAROLINA

Myrtle Beach
SOUTH CAROLINA

"RIVIERA OF THE SOUTH"
THE SWIMMING CENTER OF
THE SOUTH ATLANTIC

SC

North Carolina

South Carolina

WILMINGTON

COLUMBIA

MYRTLE
BEACH

Georgia

CHARLESTON

Savannah

93

Rapid City   174   Pierre   399
ffalo   3:29   7:53   270

GREETINGS FROM SOUTH DAKOTA

Lemon Pepper Bison Steaks

According to a journal entry from their historic expedition, in September 1804 Lewis and Clark enjoyed a buffalo cookout with a circle of Indian chiefs a few miles from Fort Pierre. The meat would have been typical feasting fare: at the time, great herds roamed miles of grasslands on the South Dakota plains, but their widespread slaughter during later decades of the nineteenth century made the animals virtually extinct by 1900. Today, a herd of some fifteen hundred bison roams Custer State Park, and a great time to visit is during the annual Buffalo Roundup in late September, when the herd is moved to corrals. Here, they are sorted; most return to the parklands, and some are sold at auction. Throughout the West, private ranches raise several hundred thousand animals for food. A low-fat meat, high in iron and protein, bison cooks much faster than beef. You'll find it packaged as "buffalo," but promoters prefer "bison": the Latin name for the North American species is *Bison bison.* Serve with Barbecued Sweet Potatoes (page 78).

Four 6-ounce buffalo steak
    medallions, about 1 inch thick

2   tablespoons olive oil

1   teaspoon garlic salt

2   teaspoons lemon pepper

Build a low fire in a charcoal grill or heat a gas grill to 325°F. Place the steaks on a platter. Brush the tops with 1 tablespoon of the olive oil and sprinkle with half of the garlic salt and lemon pepper. Turn and repeat on the other side. Oil the grill grate, add the steaks, and cook for 4 minutes on each side, turning with tongs, for medium-rare. Serve immediately.

Serves 4

THE CHUCK WAGON
CAFE

KEN and LUCYLLE VAN DUZER, Proprietors

RAPID CITY, SOUTH DAKOTA

Visit **SIOUX FALLS** *"Heart of the Great Sioux Empire"*

PRESENTED BY THE
SIOUX FALLS
SOUTH DAKOTA
Chamber of Commerce

HAPPY CHEF

THE WORLD'S LARGEST TALKING CHEF

Mitchell, SD. — I-90 & Hwy. 37 Jct.

SD

Whiskey Ribs

Tennessee is famous for its charcoal-filtered sour mash whiskey, which, like sourdough bread, uses a portion of one batch to start off the next. In 1866, Jack Daniel took a bold step and worked with the United States government to obtain permission to make whiskey; his Lynchburg establishment became the country's first licensed distillery. But liquor-making aroused fiercely independent thinkers. Prior to 1920, many small farmers across the country found it was easier to run a small still, make whiskey, and bring it to town to sell, rather than try to find a fair market for their grain crops. When Prohibition came along, residents of Appalachia proudly resisted the regulations and cleverly maintained many of their secret stills. The delicious barbecue sauce included here, which also goes well with beef, chicken, and fish, uses Tennessee whiskey. Memphis ribs, rubbed with spices and slowly cooked in a smoker, are featured at Memphis in May, a barbecue contest that attracts thousands. This recipe uses a quicker cooking method, adapted for gas or charcoal grills.

WHISKEY BARBECUE SAUCE

1	cup Tennessee whiskey (Jack Daniel's or George Dickel)
½	cup ketchup
1	cup cider vinegar
¼	cup packed brown sugar
¼	cup Worcestershire sauce
2	tablespoons hot sauce
12	pork ribs (about 4 pounds)

To make the barbecue sauce: Combine all the ingredients in a large nonreactive saucepan, bring to a boil over medium-high heat, and immediately reduce the heat to low. Simmer the mixture for 30 minutes, or until reduced by about half.

piece of foil, wrap the ribs, and crimp the foil edges to seal tightly. Turn the packet over and wrap again in the second sheet of foil.

Place the packet on the grill and cook for 15 minutes on each side. Add more coals if necessary. Oil the grill grate. With a sharp knife, slice off the foil and use tongs to lay the ribs on the grate. Brush them with the remaining sauce and cook, turning and basting every few minutes, for 8 to 10 minutes longer, or until they are sizzling and well browned. Watch carefully to be sure the ribs don't burn.

Mound the ribs onto a serving platter and put them in the middle of the table, along with ample paper napkins. Pass around corn on the cob, a green salad, and rolls.

Build a medium fire in a charcoal grill or heat a gas grill to 350°F. Lay 2 sheets of aluminum foil, each about 2 feet long, on the counter, one on top of the other. Lay the ribs down in a single layer in the middle of the foil. Drizzle ½ cup of the barbecue sauce over the ribs and use a spoon to smear it over them as evenly as possible. Bring up the edges of the top

Serves 4

97

Lone Star Beef Brisket

Texas leads the nation in the production of beef cattle—more than 14 million head per year. The industry has had a long and colorful history. In 1865, an estimated 5 million Texas longhorns roamed the open Texas ranges, and for about twenty years, starting in 1850, cattle worth as little as $5 per head at home were taken overland to California or into the Rocky Mountain goldfields, where they could sell for up to twenty times that price. One of the most beloved meals in Texas is barbecued brisket, cooked all day in a smoker and served with sauces that are well-guarded family secrets. This recipe is adapted for a backyard grill and is ready in a few hours. Serve brisket with pickles, white bread, and Coleslaw (page 116). Cut any leftovers into thin strips and reheat in the barbecue sauce.

BARBECUE SAUCE

2   tablespoons butter

1   onion, finely chopped

2   cloves garlic, minced

1   cup black coffee

1   cup ketchup

¼   cup Worcestershire sauce or steak sauce

1   tablespoon packed brown sugar

½   teaspoon red pepper flakes (optional)

1   tablespoon onion powder

2   teaspoons Hungarian paprika

Salt and freshly ground black pepper to taste

½   cup hot water, plus more as needed

1   boneless beef brisket (4 to 6 pounds)

To make the barbecue sauce: Melt the butter in a medium nonreactive saucepan over low heat. Add the onion and garlic, increase the heat to medium, and sauté until the onion is translucent, about 5 minutes. Add all the remaining sauce ingredients, stir, and simmer for 10 minutes. Remove from the heat and set aside.

Build a low fire in a charcoal grill or heat a gas grill to 325°F. With a sharp knife, trim most of the fat from the brisket, leaving a layer no more than ⅛ inch thick. Combine the onion powder, paprika, salt, and pepper in a small bowl and blend with a fork. Position the brisket in a disposable aluminum roasting pan and rub about half of the spice mixture into each side. Lay the brisket in the pan fat side up. Add the ½ cup hot water to the pan and cover it tightly with heavy-duty aluminum foil.

Place the pan on the grate, cover the grill, and cook for 1 hour, adding more coals after 30 to 45 minutes as necessary. Turn the brisket over, add a little more water to the pan, cover tightly with the foil, and cook for 1 hour longer. Add more coals to the fire after 30 to 45 minutes. Cook 3½ to 4 hours longer, turning the brisket and adding more water every hour and replenishing the coals as necessary, for a total of 4½ to 5 hours, or until the brisket shreds easily when pulled apart with a fork. Do not let the water boil away or the brisket will become dry. Remove the pan from the grill and let the brisket rest, covered with the foil, for 10 to 15 minutes. Cut the brisket into thin slices and serve topped with the barbecue sauce.

Serves 8 to 10

Dutch Oven Cherry Cobbler

In 1997, the Utah state legislature gave celebrity status to the cast-iron Dutch oven, naming it the official State Cooking Pot. The modest black three-legged pot was a fixture on nineteenth-century wagon trains, and Utah miners relied on it as well. Today, river trips and wilderness outfitters throughout the state use Dutch ovens for campfire meals, and Scout leaders teach its uses to young cooks. The International Dutch Oven Society, a nonprofit group based in Logan, publishes a newsletter and shares recipes for everything from ribs to breads. Visit their website, www.idos.com, for suppliers of authentic Dutch ovens, too. Outdoor Dutch-oven cooking requires a three-legged pot with a flat lid so that a specified number of charcoal briquettes can be used to maintain even heat on both the top and the bottom of the oven. Here's an easy recipe, developed by the 2004 World Champion Dutch Oven Cooks. It's designed for a casual backyard family get-together. Serve with whipped cream or vanilla ice cream.

Two 12½-ounce cans unsweetened dark sweet cherries (see note)
1 cup packed brown sugar
2 cups all-purpose flour
1 cup granulated sugar
2 teaspoons baking powder
2 teaspoons poppy seeds
1 egg, beaten
½ cup (1 stick) butter

Build a medium fire in a charcoal grill, using about 26 charcoal briquettes.

Drain the cherries and reserve the juice. Combine the cherries and brown sugar in a small bowl and set aside. Combine the flour, granulated sugar, baking powder, and poppy seeds in a medium bowl. Stir to blend well. Stir in the egg and about ¾ cup of the reserved cherry juice to make a fairly thick batter. If necessary, add a little more juice so you can just stir the heavy batter with a spoon.

Make a bed with 7 or 8 of the lighted briquettes and set a 12-inch Dutch oven on top. Add the butter and let it melt. Spoon the batter as evenly as possible on top of the melted butter. (The butter will come up over the batter at the edges.) Gently spoon the sweetened cherries and any juice remaining in the bowl into the center of the batter. Cover the pan and add 16 to 18 briquettes to the top of the lid. Bake for 45 minutes to 1 hour, rotating the oven every 15 minutes to redistribute the heat. Don't peek under the lid for at least 30 minutes. The cobbler is done when the sides just begin to pull away from the pan and a knife or toothpick inserted in the center comes out clean.

With a serving spoon, scoop the hot cobbler into dessert bowls and top with whipped cream or vanilla ice cream.

Serves 8 to 10

Note: If you can find only sweetened canned cherries, use ½ cup brown sugar and ½ cup granulated sugar in the recipe. If it rains, or if you have a flat-bottomed Dutch oven, bake the cobbler in a preheated 350°F oven for about 45 minutes, with a baking sheet under the Dutch oven to diffuse the heat.

Sugar Loaf Cafe – St. George, Utah

Oven-Baked Maple Barbecue Chicken Wings

The small state of Vermont is the largest producer of maple syrup in the United States. Depending on the weather, the four-to-six-week sugaring season can start as early as February in the southern part of the state and last until late April in the north. Seasonal celebrations to mark sugaring time include the Vermont Maple Festival, which is held in St. Albans on the last weekend in April and demonstrates the many culinary uses of maple syrup. The no-nonsense, tasty sauce included here was developed by the festival chairman. The authentic version uses maple vinegar, which is sold at the event, but cider vinegar works as well. Brush some of the sauce on grilled meat or chicken during the last few minutes of cooking, being very careful not to let it burn. Or, use it for these oven-baked wings, which make a terrific appetizer to serve while the grill is heating. Kids will devour them.

½ cup homemade or bottled barbecue sauce (any brand)

¼ cup pure maple syrup

¼ cup maple vinegar or cider vinegar

4 pounds chicken wings

Heat the broiler. Combine the barbecue sauce, maple syrup, and vinegar in a small nonreactive bowl and thoroughly blend with a whisk. Arrange the wings on a broiler pan and cook 8 to 12 inches from the heat source for 5 minutes. Turn with tongs, brush with some of the sauce, and continue cooking, turning and brushing with more of the sauce, for 20 minutes longer, or until the wings are browned and sizzling but not blackened. Serve warm, with plenty of paper napkins for sticky fingers.

Serves 6 to 8

KENTUCKY
331
7:35
Richmond
99
2:01
Norfolk

GREETINGS FROM

VIRGINIA

THE OLD DOMINION STATE

Pineapple-Glazed Ham

When colonists from England settled Jamestown, they brought along pigs, which flourished in the temperate climate. Adapting the techniques of smoking and salting used by the Indians, the settlers devised methods for curing hams and built smokehouses to give them delicious and distinctive flavor. Salty dry-cured country hams, which keep without refrigeration, are a signature state product. One venerable ham, cured in 1902, is on display at the Isle of Wight Museum in Smithfield. This recipe uses a precooked ham slice. Serve with applesauce and Corn Muffins (page 121).

One 2-pound ham slice, about
    1 inch thick
1   cup pineapple juice
6   whole cloves

PINEAPPLE GLAZE
¼   cup pineapple jam (see note)
1   tablespoon Dijon mustard
¼   teaspoon ground cloves

The night before grilling, put the ham slice in a shallow nonreactive dish and pour the pineapple juice over it. Scatter the cloves on top. Turn the ham slice, cover it with plastic wrap, and refrigerate overnight, turning once or twice.

Build a medium fire in a charcoal grill or heat a gas grill to 350°F.

To make the pineapple glaze: Combine all the ingredients in a small nonreactive saucepan and cook over medium heat until the mixture bubbles, stirring until smooth. Reduce the heat to low and cook, stirring frequently, for 10 minutes, or until the mixture is slightly thickened.

Oil the grill grate. Remove the ham from the marinade and place it on the grate. Discard the marinade. Cook the ham for 5 minutes. Brush the top with some of the glaze, turn, and cook for 5 minutes longer. Brush the top with the

remaining glaze, turn, and cook 3 minutes
longer, or until the bottom is browned and
bubbling. Serve immediately.

Serves 4 to 6

Note: If you can't find pineapple jam,
use apricot jam.

Planked Salmon

Although farmed salmon is easy to find in most markets and restaurants, the lure of wild salmon from the Pacific Northwest attracts fishermen from around the world. If you find yourself with a big piece of salmon, farmed or wild, give plank grilling a try. It's a great way to cook this meaty fish, which can otherwise stick to the grill and flake apart when you try to remove it. Cedar is aromatic and gives a wonderful flavor to salmon. Culinary legend has it that the technique of cooking salmon on wood dates back to the coastal tribes of the Northwest. You can buy planks packaged for grilling at kitchen stores or online, or visit your local hardware store and buy a piece of untreated construction-grade cedar (see note). Serve the salmon with sautéed asparagus and Mom's Potato Salad (page 117).

One 2- to 2½-pound salmon fillet with skin

3 tablespoons olive oil, plus more for oiling plank

1 tablespoon minced fresh rosemary, or 1 teaspoon dried rosemary

Salt and freshly ground black pepper to taste

Put an 8-by-14-inch cedar plank in a large roasting pan and add water to cover. Weigh the plank down with a heavy can or stone to keep it submerged and soak for 30 minutes.

Build a medium-hot fire in a charcoal grill or heat a gas grill to 375°F. Pat the salmon dry with paper towels and place it on a large platter, skin side up. Rub the skin with 1 tablespoon of the olive oil and turn it over. Combine the remaining 2 tablespoons olive oil and the rosemary in a small bowl and rub the mixture on the salmon, sprinkling it to taste with salt and pepper. Remove the cedar plank from the water and oil it. Place the salmon on the plank, skin side down.

Put the plank in the center of the grill grate, cover the grill, open the lid vents halfway, and cook until the salmon flakes easily with a fork, about 20 minutes. (The plank may smoke and get charred; that's okay.)

Wearing oven mitts, remove the plank from the grill and set it down on a heatproof surface. Using a spatula, cut the salmon into serving-size pieces and arrange them on dinner plates with the asparagus and potato salad.

Serves 4 to 6

Note: Lumberyards sell 1-by-8-inch cedar boards in lengths of 8 to 10 feet, ranging from $3 to $4 per board foot. If your lumberyard doesn't offer custom cutting, ask for a 2-foot length and cut it down at home, or buy a larger piece and plan for several plank-grilling meals. Remember to measure your grill before you go shopping for planks so you don't bring home one that is too long to fit.

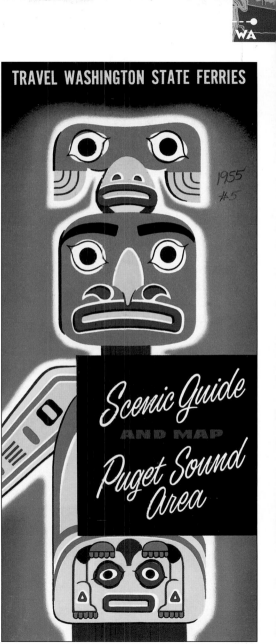

TRAVEL WASHINGTON STATE FERRIES

Scenic Guide AND MAP *Puget Sound Area*

Grilled Trout with Spinach-Ramp Stuffing

Ramps, or wild leeks, grow in the upper elevations of the Appalachian woodlands. They're the first green to appear in the spring, and they're celebrated at April festivals in Morgantown, Elkins, and Richwood, West Virginia, among other communities, for heralding a new season as well as for their distinctive taste, a bit like a marriage of onions and garlic. Although ramps turn up in East and West Coast city markets in April and May, selling for a shocking $10 to $12 a pound, the earlier they are dug and the less time they sit around, the milder they taste. Here, they're paired with trout, another Appalachian treat. Substitute ½ cup chopped leeks and 2 minced garlic cloves if you can't find ramps, and buy farmed trout if you can't get to West Virginia to do some fishing. Serve with Corn Muffins (page 121) and a green salad.

SPINACH-RAMP STUFFING

4   tablespoons olive oil

½   cup chopped ramps (6 to 8 ramps, white part only)

2   cups packed chopped spinach

1   cup fresh bread crumbs

¼   cup grated Parmesan cheese

Salt and freshly ground black pepper to taste

4   whole trout (about 12 ounces each)

Olive oil for coating

Salt and freshly ground black pepper to taste

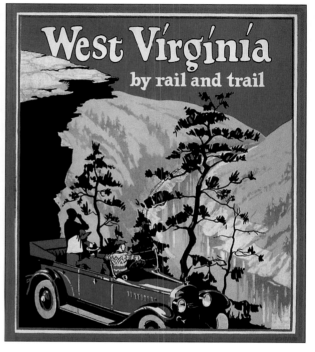

Build a medium fire in a charcoal grill or heat a gas grill to 350°F.

To make the spinach-ramp stuffing:
Heat 2 tablespoons of the olive oil in a small skillet over medium-low heat and sauté the ramps for 5 minutes, or until they are soft and fragrant. Stir in the spinach and cook for 5 minutes, stirring frequently, until it is wilted. Add the bread crumbs and cook, stirring, for 1 to 2 minutes, until they are well mixed with the other ingredients. Add the cheese and stir again. Season with salt and pepper and drizzle with the remaining 2 tablespoons olive oil. Stir to mix well and remove from the heat.

Pat the trout dry with paper towels, coat with a little olive oil, and season with salt and pepper. Spoon one-fourth of the stuffing into each trout cavity and press the edges together. Place the trout in an oiled grilling basket. Place the basket on the grate and cook the trout for 5 minutes on each side, or until the flesh flakes easily with a fork. Using a spatula, gently transfer each trout onto a dinner plate. Pass the salad and muffins.

Serves 4

Grilled Brats

When German immigrants settled in Wisconsin in the nineteenth century, they brought along the
sausage-making traditions that have
been kept very much alive in many
parts of the state. The bratwurst, a
spicy pork sausage, reigns supreme.
It's grilled at fund-raisers and summer cookouts referred to as "brat
fries." Sheboygan hosts an annual
Bratwurst Day the first Saturday in
August, and in Milwaukee, Usinger's,

a meat market in operation since
1880, is legendary for their sausages.
Come summer, brats are the food to
cook on the grill. The rule of thumb
is to put them on to cook, enjoy two
beers, and they're done. You don't have
to serve them sandwich style, but
that's the most popular way to enjoy
them, along with German Potato
Salad (page 117) and New England
Baked Beans (page 120). To eat brats
Sheboygan style, put two in one bun.

10 **bratwurst sausages (about
2 pounds)**

2 **onions, chopped**

2 **cans beer**

10 **crusty kaiser-style rolls,
split in half**

Brown mustard for serving

Build a medium fire in a charcoal grill or heat
a gas grill to 350°F. Meanwhile, put the brats
in a large pot, add the onions and beer, and
enough water so the brats are covered. Bring
just to a simmer over medium heat. Reduce
the heat to medium-low and simmer gently for
15 to 20 minutes. Don't let the liquid boil, or
the brats might burst.

Using tongs, remove the brats from the water.
Oil the grill grate, add the brats, and cook,
turning every few minutes with the tongs, for
10 to 15 minutes, or until nicely browned and
sizzling. Put the brats in the rolls and serve
immediately, with the mustard alongside.

Serves 5 to 10

Old Faithful
296
MONTANA
WYOMING

Grilled Spiced Elk Tenderloin

When Wyoming Territory became a state in 1890, the country around Jackson Hole was virtually unsettled. Thousands of elk ranged there. But as ranchers arrived, they claimed much of the land, and in winter, especially during the heavy snows from 1909 to 1911, the hay they put out for their cows attracted hungry elk. In response to the problem, as early as 1910 the U.S. government bought up land to separate the elk and feed them through the winter. Today, this area, which covers almost twenty-five thousand acres, is called the National Elk Refuge. From October to May, close to seventy-five hundred elk spend the winter here. (The movie *Shane* was filmed on the refuge's expansive, open stretches.) An estimated one hundred and fifty thousand elk are currently farmed in the United States today. Their low-fat meat is prized for its rich flavor. The tenderloin, a chef's favorite cut, becomes magical when grilled. Cut into slices and serve with roasted onions and peppers.

SPICE MIX

- 1½ teaspoons freshly ground black pepper
- 1½ teaspoons ground allspice
- 1 teaspoon salt
- ¾ teaspoon ground cinnamon
- ¾ teaspoon ground cloves
- ½ teaspoon ground nutmeg
- 1 tablespoon olive oil

- 1 elk tenderloin (1 to 1½ pounds)

Build a medium fire in a charcoal grill or heat a gas grill to 350°F.

To make the spice mix: Combine all the dry ingredients in a small bowl and blend with a whisk. Add the olive oil and whisk to make a smooth paste. Rub the paste evenly over the entire tenderloin and set it aside.

Oil the grill grate. Place the tenderloin on the grate and cook, turning every 3 or 4 minutes, for a total of 12 to 14 minutes, or until the meat reaches 145°F to 150°F on an instant-read thermometer. Remove from the grill and let rest for 5 minutes before slicing.

Serves **3** to **4**

Cookout Favorites

When you're planning a cookout, be sure to include some old standbys: cold salads, fruit dishes, and desserts that travel well and remind everyone of being a kid. Here's a selection of summertime specials to round out your menu, whether you're on the road or entertaining in the backyard.

SPARKLING LEMONADE

For more than a century, lemonade has been served at American summer gatherings. To get that nostalgic real taste, you need to do more than reach for a can from the freezer. Here's a recipe inspired by the legendary lemonade served at New York's City Bakery.

⅔ **cup sugar**
2 **cups fresh lemon juice**
3 **cups cold sparkling water**
Ice cubes for serving

Combine the sugar and lemon juice in a glass pitcher and stir until the sugar dissolves. Cover with plastic wrap and refrigerate for at least 1 hour. To serve, add the sparkling water and pour into tall, ice-filled glasses.

Serves 4

CITRUS ICED TEA

Here's a deliciously different iced tea, inspired by the popular Southern flavors of mint and orange. Allow at least 4 hours for the flavors to mingle.

6 **cups water**
8 **Earl Grey tea bags**
3 **tablespoons confectioners' sugar**
10 **sprigs mint**
1 **cup fresh orange juice**
Juice of 1 lime (about 3 tablespoons)
Ice cubes for serving
1 **lemon, sliced**

Bring the water to a boil in a large stainless-steel saucepan, remove from the heat, add the tea bags, and let steep for 10 minutes, or until the tea looks strong. Remove the tea bags and add the sugar and half the mint. Let stand for 30 minutes. Remove the mint. Add the orange and lime juices, pour into a pitcher, cover with plastic wrap, and refrigerate for at least 1 hour or up to 4 hours. To serve, fill a large pitcher with ice and pour in the tea mixture along with the remaining mint sprigs and the lemon slices. Stir and pour into ice-filled glasses.

Serves 8 to 10

FRESH VEGGIE PLATTER WITH HUMMUS

If you want to serve an easy and healthful appetizer at your next cookout, take a little time to assemble a large platter of fresh raw vegetables with your own homemade chickpea dip. Add a basket of sliced pita bread or corn chips and watch it all disappear.

HUMMUS

1   can (19 ounces) chickpeas (garbanzo beans), rinsed and drained

¼   cup olive oil

½   cup tahini

Juice of 1 lemon

2   to 3 scallions, white part only, diced

½   cup chopped fresh flat-leaf parsley

Salt to taste

1   bag (1 pound) peeled baby carrots

2   cups cherry tomatoes

2   red bell peppers, seeded and cut into 1-inch-wide strips

2   yellow bell peppers, seeded and cut into 1-inch-wide strips

1   small head broccoli, cut into florets

1   small head cauliflower, cut into florets

4   cucumbers, peeled and sliced

4   stalks celery, cut into 3-inch sticks

2   fennel bulbs, trimmed and cut diagonally into thin slices

To make the hummus: Combine all the ingredients except the parsley and salt in a food processor and process for 3 minutes, or until the mixture is smooth and creamy. Spoon into a small nonreactive bowl, stir in the parsley, and season with salt.

Arrange the vegetables in rows on a large platter and set the hummus in the center. To prepare ahead, cover with plastic wrap and refrigerate for up to 4 hours.

Serves 10 to 12

TABBOULEH

This Middle Eastern grain salad, especially refreshing on a hot day, is always appreciated by guests who are cutting back on meat or trying not to fill up on chips and bread. Add diced tomatoes or olives if you wish.

1½ **cups water**

1 **cup coarse bulgur wheat**

1 **teaspoon salt, plus salt to taste**

Juice of 1 lemon or lime (about ¼ cup)

2 **to 3 cloves garlic, minced**

¼ **cup olive oil**

1 **cucumber, peeled, seeded, and minced**

1 **cup minced fresh flat-leaf parsley**

Freshly ground black pepper to taste

Bring the water to a boil in a medium nonreactive saucepan and stir in the bulgur and the 1 teaspoon salt. Remove from the heat, cover, and let stand for 30 minutes, or until all the water is absorbed. Add the lemon juice, garlic, and olive oil and stir gently to mix. Transfer the bulgur to a medium nonreactive bowl. Cover with plastic wrap and refrigerate for at least 1 hour or up to 8 hours. To serve, add the cucumber and parsley, and season with salt and pepper to taste.

Serves 6 to 8

COLESLAW

You can find this popular cabbage salad ready-made at just about every supermarket deli in America, but the kind you prepare yourself will have better flavor and texture than anything you can buy. This version is colorful and crunchy. You can shred cabbage in a food processor, but it ends up being very fine and tends to get soggy quickly. For best results, use a sharp knife. Serve with just about any grilled food as a side dish, or tuck it into hamburgers and other sandwiches. Since it contains mayonnaise, don't leave it out on hot days; carry it to and from a picnic in a cooler.

1 **small green cabbage (about 1½ pounds)**

1 **small red cabbage (about 12 ounces)**

4 **carrots, peeled and shredded**

DRESSING

½ **cup mayonnaise**

½ **cup sour cream or plain yogurt**

1 **tablespoon white balsamic vinegar**

1 **teaspoon sugar**

1 **to 2 teaspoons celery seed**

Cut each cabbage into quarters, remove the cores, and lay the wedges flat on a cutting board. Slice into thin shreds and cut the shreds in half lengthwise. (You will have about 10 to 12 cups shredded cabbage.) Put the cabbage in a large nonreactive bowl and add the carrots.

To make the dressing: Combine all the ingredients in a small nonreactive bowl and blend with a whisk until smooth. Pour the mixture over the cabbage and toss gently with a spoon until well mixed. Cover with plastic wrap and refrigerate for at least 1 hour or up to 4 hours before serving.

Serves 10 to 12

MOM'S POTATO SALAD

Be careful if you decide to deviate from tradition when you make a batch of potato salad for a family party. If your mother always added hard-cooked eggs, do the same. To cut back on the calories, use half mayonnaise and half plain yogurt.

2   to 3 pounds unpeeled potatoes, preferably Yukon Gold

Salt and freshly ground black pepper to taste

¼   **cup olive oil**

2   **tablespoons cider vinegar**

3   **hard-cooked eggs, chopped (optional)**

¼   **cup chopped fresh flat-leaf parsley or dill**

¼   **cup chopped fresh chives or scallions (white part only)**

2   **to 3 stalks celery, finely chopped**

½   **to 1 cup mayonnaise**

Put the potatoes in a large stockpot of water, bring to a boil, reduce the heat to medium, and simmer for 15 minutes, or until fork-tender. (Or, steam them, in batches if necessary, over 2 inches of water in a covered large pan for 8 minutes.) Drain and let cool just enough to

handle. While they are still warm, peel the potatoes and cut them into chunks as large or small as you like. Season with salt and pepper. Combine the olive oil and vinegar in a small nonreactive bowl and whisk until smooth. Pour the mixture over the potatoes and toss gently. Add the hard-cooked eggs, if using, and the parsley, chives, and celery. Add just enough mayonnaise to moisten the potatoes. Toss the mixture gently with a rubber spatula. Season with salt and pepper to taste and serve. To prepare ahead, cover with plastic wrap and refrigerate for up to 8 hours. Transport to a picnic in a cooler.

Serves 6 to 8

GERMAN POTATO SALAD

Serve this salad hot, cold, or at room temperature. The bacon fat makes it authentic, but if you must, drain off all the bacon fat and substitute 2 tablespoons of butter to make the sauce.

5   **pounds unpeeled small red potatoes**

12   **ounces bacon, cut into ½-inch pieces**

1   **large onion, chopped**

2   **tablespoons all-purpose flour**

¾   **cup apple cider vinegar**

2   **cups water**

¼   **cup sugar**

Salt to taste, plus 2 teaspoons

Freshly ground black pepper to taste

5   **stalks celery, chopped**

continued

Put the potatoes in a large pot of water and bring to a boil over high heat. Reduce the heat to medium and simmer for 20 minutes, or until the potatoes are fork-tender.

While the potatoes are cooking, fry the bacon in a large nonreactive skillet over medium heat, stirring frequently, for about 10 minutes, or until crisp. Using a slotted spoon, transfer the bacon to paper towels to drain. Pour off all but about 2 tablespoons of fat from the pan. Add the onion and sauté over medium-low heat for 5 minutes, or until translucent. Add the flour and stir for several minutes, until the flour starts to brown. Add the vinegar, water, and sugar. Reduce the heat to low and cook the sauce for about 5 minutes, stirring frequently, until it thickens. Season with salt and pepper to taste.

Peel and slice the potatoes while they are still hot and place them in a large bowl. Sprinkle with the 2 teaspoons salt. Add the cooked bacon, and celery. Pour the sauce over the top and stir gently until well mixed.

Serves 8 to 10

PASTA SALAD

Give this salad some backbone by using the sturdier rotelli or fusilli in place of macaroni. You can add just about anything you wish—chopped marinated or fresh vegetables, a variety of herbs, or slices or chunks of cooked meat or chicken—to make it more substantial.

2	**cups rotelli or fusilli pasta**
2	**teaspoons plus 5 tablespoons olive oil**
3	**tablespoons white balsamic vinegar**
1	**tablespoon Dijon mustard**
1	**tablespoon minced fresh tarragon, or 1 teaspoon dried tarragon**
1	**red bell pepper, seeded and diced**
½	**cup pitted kalamata olives**
½	**cup crumbled feta cheese**
1	**jar (6 ounces) marinated artichoke hearts, drained**

Cook the pasta in a large pot of boiling water, stirring occasionally with a wooden spoon, for 6 to 8 minutes, or until al dente (tender but still firm). Immediately drain in a colander, return to the pot, and gently toss with the 2 teaspoons olive oil. Spread it out on a large baking sheet to cool. (To make up to 24 hours ahead, spoon the cooled pasta into a bowl and cover with plastic wrap until you're ready to assemble the salad.)

Put the cooked and cooled pasta in a large nonreactive bowl. Combine the 5 tablespoons olive oil, vinegar, mustard, and tarragon in a glass jar with a tight-fitting lid and shake until smooth. Pour the dressing over the pasta and toss gently. Add the remaining ingredients and toss again.

Serves 4 to 6

THREE-BEAN SALAD

A staple of the picnic table, this classic salad is easy to make and a favorite with all ages. If you buy it from a deli, it's often soggy and loaded with sugar. Make your own to enjoy a rich, beany crunch.

¼ **cup cider vinegar**

½ **cup olive oil**

¼ **teaspoon dry mustard**

Salt and freshly ground black pepper to taste

8 **ounces green beans, cut into 2-inch pieces**

8 **ounces wax (yellow) beans, cut into 2-inch pieces**

1 **can (16 ounces) red kidney beans, rinsed and drained**

1 **small red onion, diced**

1 **large red or green bell pepper, seeded and diced**

¼ **cup chopped fresh flat-leaf parsley**

Combine the vinegar, olive oil, mustard, salt, and pepper in a large nonreactive bowl and whisk until smooth. Cook the fresh green and yellow beans in a large pot of salted boiling water for about 5 minutes, or until crisp-tender. Drain and add to the dressing in the bowl, along with the remaining ingredients. Toss gently. Taste and adjust the seasoning. Cover with plastic wrap and refrigerate for at least 2 hours or up to 8 hours.

Serves 6

RANCH BEANS

Dried beans were an important chuck wagon staple. Easy to carry, inexpensive, and filling, they could be tossed in a pot and cooked over an open fire with whatever other ingredients were at hand. At the annual World Championship Chuckwagon Roundup held each June in Amarillo, Texas, each wagon must cook four gallons of pinto beans, along with panfried steak, white gravy, potatoes, and sourdough biscuits, over an open fire. You can bake these beans on your stove top.

1 **pound dried pinto beans**

4 **ounces salt pork or bacon, diced**

2 **onions, chopped**

3 **large cloves garlic, minced**

3 **jalapeño chilies, seeded and minced**

2 **tablespoons chili powder**

½ **teaspoon freshly ground black pepper**

Salt to taste

Hot sauce to taste (optional)

Rinse the beans in a colander and sort through, picking out any that are shriveled. Put the beans in a large pot, add cold water to cover, and let them soak overnight. The next day, drain the beans in a colander and rinse again.

Put the salt pork in the pot and cook over medium heat, stirring with a wooden spoon, until it starts to brown, about 5 minutes. Add the onions, garlic, and jalapeños and sauté over medium heat until soft, about 4 minutes.
continued

Stir in the chili powder and pepper and cook 1 minute longer. Add the beans and enough cold water to just cover them. Stir well. Increase the heat to high and bring the mixture to a boil. Reduce the heat to low and let the beans simmer, uncovered, for 5 to 6 hours, or until tender but not mushy. Stir occasionally and add more water as necessary to keep them from sticking. Season with salt before serving. If they're not spicy enough for your taste, season them with your favorite hot sauce.

Serves 10 to 12

NEW ENGLAND BAKED BEANS

Unlike unsweetened ranch beans, this dish is traditionally flavored with brown sugar or molasses, or both. The taste depends on the type of dried beans you use; the delicious varieties listed below are sold online and at natural foods stores. If you can't find them, use navy or pinto beans. Serve these beans hot or cold. They'll keep warm for hours in a slow cooker.

1	**pound dried beans, preferably Jacob's Cattle, Yellow Eye, or Soldier beans**
1	**teaspoon salt**
2	**tablespoons dry mustard**
½	**teaspoon ground ginger**
4	**tablespoons blackstrap molasses**
8	**ounces bacon, diced**

Rinse the beans in a colander and sort through, picking out any that are shriveled. Put the beans in a large pot, add cold water to cover, and soak overnight. The next day, drain the beans in a colander and rinse again. Return the beans to the pot, cover with water, and bring to a boil over high heat. Immediately reduce the heat to low and simmer the beans, uncovered, for 2 hours. Check once or twice to be sure they are just barely covered with water.

Heat the oven to 200°F. Add the salt, mustard, ginger, and molasses to the beans and stir gently to mix. Put half the bacon pieces in an 8-cup ovenproof casserole. Spoon the beans on top of the bacon and add the remaining bacon pieces on top. Add water to barely cover the beans. Cover and bake for 10 hours, or until the beans are tender. Check the beans several times during cooking and add more water if needed.

Serves 6 to 8

CORN MUFFINS

Portable as well as versatile, these muffins go nicely with barbecued chicken, grilled steaks, fish, and vegetable dinners. The brown sugar gives them a special flavor. Serve with honey and butter.

1   cup yellow cornmeal
1   cup all-purpose flour
2½   teaspoons baking powder
½   teaspoon salt
4   tablespoons butter, melted
½   cup packed light brown sugar
1   large egg
1   cup milk

Heat the oven to 400°F. Grease a 12-cup muffin pan.

Combine the cornmeal, flour, baking powder, and salt in a medium bowl and stir with a whisk to blend. Combine the melted butter, brown sugar, egg, and milk in a second medium bowl and whisk until smooth. Add the dry ingredients to the wet and slowly stir with a spoon until the dry ingredients are moistened. Spoon the batter into the prepared muffin cups and bake for 20 minutes, or until the edges of the muffins are slightly browned and the tops feel firm when you press them gently.

Makes 12

FRUIT-FILLED WATERMELON BASKET

This charming summer fruit salad never goes out of style. One sign of a good, ripe watermelon is a yellow underbelly; use that side as the bottom of your basket. If the watermelon is tippy, cut a very thin slice off the bottom to make it level. After cutting the melon in half lengthwise, use a small, sharp knife to cut a sawtooth edge all around the outside of the basket half.

1 large watermelon, preferably oblong
1 cantaloupe
1 honeydew melon
1 pineapple
2 cups fresh blueberries or strawberries
2 tablespoons fresh lime juice

With a large, sharp knife, cut the watermelon lengthwise to remove the top third. Set this aside for another use. (If you want to leave a "handle," make 2 cuts, one from the left side and one from the right, and stop on either side about 1 inch before you get to the center. Then cut straight down from the top and remove the 2 top wedges. Hollow out the flesh underneath the handle.)

Working carefully with a smaller knife—a grapefruit knife is ideal—slice all around the edge of the watermelon to a depth of about 4 inches, leaving about ¼ inch of pink flesh and
continued

being careful not to puncture the rind. Gently cut out long, 1-inch-thick slices of watermelon. Cut the slices as evenly as you can into 1-inch cubes and put them in a large bowl. Keep a fork at the ready and use it to remove seeds as you come across them. Continue working until the watermelon is hollowed out. To make ahead, cover the watermelon basket and the bowl of watermelon cubes with plastic wrap and refrigerate for up to 4 hours. Drain the watermelon before proceeding.

Just before serving, cut the cantaloupe and honeydew melon in half and scoop out the seeds. With a sharp knife, cut the melons lengthwise into sections about 1 inch thick. Peel and slice the flesh into chunks. Put the pieces in a large nonreactive bowl. Stand the pineapple upright and cut off the rind. Cut it in half lengthwise, then cut each piece in half lengthwise. Remove the core and cut the quarters into chunks. Add to the bowl. Add the blueberries, if using. If using strawberries, remove the hulls and slice the berries into the bowl. Remove the watermelon cubes from the refrigerator, drain, and add to the bowl. Sprinkle the fruit with the lime juice and toss gently.

Spoon the fruit into the chilled basket and serve with a slotted spoon. (If you're carrying the basket to a party where it won't be served for several hours, keep the fruit in the bowl and take the basket separately. When you get to the party, use the slotted spoon to transfer the fruit to the basket.)

Serves 10 to 12

RED, WHITE, AND BLUE CHEESECAKE

This simple cheesecake without a crust makes a great summertime dessert. For a Fourth of July party, bake it in a rectangular pan and arrange the berries to look like the American flag. Make it a day or two in advance. Both the low baking temperature and the steam from the pan of water you put in the oven will help prevent cracking, but cheesecake can have a mind of its own. If a crack does form, simply hide it with the sour cream.

1½ **pounds cream cheese (three 8-ounce packages) at room temperature**
1 **cup sugar**
3 **eggs**
1 **teaspoon vanilla extract**
3 **tablespoons all-purpose flour**
1 **cup heavy cream**
1 **cup sour cream**
2 **cups ripe fresh strawberries or raspberries**
1 **cup fresh blueberries**

Heat the oven to 325°F. Generously butter a 7-by-11-inch baking pan. In the bowl of an electric mixer or in a food processor, cream the softened cream cheese. With the machine running, gradually add the sugar and eggs, then the vanilla, flour, and heavy cream, beating or blending for about 1 minute, or just until smooth.

Pour the batter into the prepared pan and set on the middle rack in the oven. Set a large roasting pan containing about 1 inch of hot water on a lower rack, underneath the pan. Bake for 45 minutes, or until the cake is lightly browned and the center jiggles only slightly when you gently shake the pan.

Turn off the oven but leave the cake in it for about 20 minutes longer, so it cools gradually. Remove from the oven, cover with plastic wrap, and refrigerate for at least 2 hours or up to 8 hours. To serve, spread the sour cream over the top. Hull and slice the strawberries, if using. To simulate red stripes, arrange the berries, just barely overlapping, in rows. Put the blueberries in a square in the upper left-hand corner.

Serves 10 to 12

PERFECT PICNIC CUPCAKES

Tasty and easy to make, cupcakes are the ideal traveling dessert, requiring no forks or plates. If you're celebrating a birthday, put a candle in each one and stack them in several layers.

2   cups all-purpose flour
1   teaspoon baking powder
1   cup sugar
½   cup (1 stick) butter at room temperature
3   eggs
1   teaspoon vanilla extract
½   cup milk

CHOCOLATE FROSTING

4   tablespoons butter
½   cup heavy cream
2   tablespoons unsweetened cocoa powder
2   cups confectioners' sugar

Heat the oven to 375°F. Line a 12 muffin cup pan with paper baking liners. Combine the flour and baking powder in a small bowl and stir with a whisk to blend. Set aside. Combine the sugar and butter in the bowl of an electric mixer and beat on medium speed for several minutes until the mixture is smooth. Beat in the eggs, one at a time, then the vanilla. Alternately add the flour mixture and the milk in several additions and beat for several minutes until the batter is smooth and pale. Spoon the batter evenly into the baking cups, filling them about two-thirds full. Bake for 15 to 20 minutes, or until the tops are very lightly browned and spring back when you press them gently with a finger. Transfer the pan to a wire rack and let cool slightly.

To make the chocolate frosting: Combine the butter, cream, and cocoa powder in a medium saucepan and cook over low heat, stirring frequently, for about 5 minutes, or until the butter melts and the mixture is smooth. Add the confectioners' sugar and stir until smooth. Frost the cupcakes while they are still warm.

Makes 12

RECIPE PERMISSIONS

ALASKA: Spicy Grilled Chili-Lime Halibut (page 14). Used by permission of Jeff Riggs, Fisherman's Express.

IDAHO: Crispy Idaho Potato Wedges (page 34). Used by permission of Idaho Potato Commission.

INDIANA: Beer Can Chicken (page 38). Used by permission of Chris Coburn, www.coltsfanbulance.com.

IOWA: Fruit-Stuffed Iowa Chops with Apple-Pecan Sauce (page 40). Used by permission of Lew Miller, founder of Iowa BBQ Society and former Iowa State Fair Cook-Off King.

KANSAS: KSU Barbecued Chicken (page 42). Used by permission of Scott Beyer, Kansas State University Agricultural Experiment Station and Cooperative Extension Service.

MINNESOTA: Grilled Steak with Peach Salsa (page 58). Used by permission of Minnesota Beef Council.

MISSOURI: Kansas City Ribs (page 62). Used by permission of Dan Cherrington, www.kansascity cooking.com.

NEBRASKA: Grilled Pot Roast Pipérade (page 66). Used by permission of Cattlemen's Beef Board and National Cattlemen's Beef Association.

NEW MEXICO: Grilled Green Chili–Stuffed Pepper Steaks (page 74). Used by permission of Dave Dewitt and Nancy Gerlach, Fiery-Foods and Barbecue Supersite, www.fiery-foods.com.

PENNSYLVANIA: South Philly Hamburgers (page 88). Used by permission of Alan B. Eastep, Alan's Kitchen, www.alanskitchen.com.

UTAH: Dutch Oven Cherry Cobbler (page 100). Used by permission of Vickie and Bruce Tracy, International Dutch Oven Society, www.idos.com.

VERMONT: Oven-Baked Maple Barbecue Chicken Wings (page 102). Used by permission of Jim Cameron, chairman of the Vermont Maple Festival.

WYOMING: Grilled Spiced Elk Tenderloin (page 112). Used by permission of Rich Forrest, Grande Premium Meat, www.elkusa.com.

GERMAN POTATO SALAD (page 117). Used by permission of Jim Schroeder, The Bratwurst Pages, www.bratwurst pages.com.

RED, WHITE, AND BLUE CHEESECAKE (page 122). Used by permission of Cynthia Van Hazinga, Waverly Research Center, New York, NY.

ILLUSTRATION CREDITS

Cover: *How To Be a Cookout Champion* booklet cover, ©1959 Kaiser Aluminum & Chemical Corp., courtesy of Kaiser Aluminum; Jim Heimann Collection.

1. Chrome postcard, ca. 1960s, Don and Newly Preziosi Collection.

3. Magazine advertisement detail, 1957, courtesy Leland and Crystal Payton.

6. Chrome postcard, ca. 1959.

7. Magazine advertisement, ca. 1960, courtesy Leland and Crystal Payton.

8. Magazine advertisement detail, 1960, courtesy Leland and Crystal Payton.

9. Chrome postcard, ca. 1960, Don and Newly Preziosi Collection.

10. Chrome postcard, ca. 1960, Don and Newly Preziosi Collection.

11. Chrome postcard, ca. 1960, Don and Newly Preziosi Collection.

12. Large-letter linen postcard, ca. 1940.

13. (left) *Cook-out Recipes* booklet, ca. 1950s, Jim Heimann Collection; (right) *Alabama Vacation Trails*, travel booklet, ca. 1940s.

14. Large-letter linen postcard, 1942.

15. *Alaska and the Yukon*, travel booklet, 1935.

16. Large-letter linen postcard, 1942.

17. *Mesa Arizona*, travel booklet, ca. 1940s.

18. (top) Large-letter linen postcard, ca. 1940s; (bottom) White Pig Bar-B-Q matchbook cover, ca. 1940.

19. (left) Maurice Bessinger's Flying Pig sign, West Columbia, SC, photograph ©1988 John Margolies/Esto; (right) *Meet Me at Hot Springs National Park Arkansas*, ca. 1930s.

20. Large-letter linen postcard, 1938.

21. Linen postcard, 1942.

22. (top) Large-letter linen postcard, 1945; (bottom) illustration from *Big Boy Barbecue Book* ©1956, 1957 by Tested Recipe Institute, Inc., Jim Heimann Collection.

23. (left) *Come to Colorado Springs-Manito, The Pikes Peak Region*, travel booklet, ca. 1920s; (right) *Colorado Vacations*, travel brochure, 1934.

24. Large-letter linen postcard, 1940.

25. (left) Real photo postcard, Clam Beach, CA, ca. 1940s; (right) linen postcard, ca. 1940s.

26. Large-letter linen postcard, 1939.

27. (top) *Rehoboth Beach Delaware*, travel booklet, 1932; (bottom) drawing from Tropical Restaurant, Brunswick, GA, double-fold postcard, ca. 1940s; (right) illustration from *Big Boy Barbecue Book* ©1956, 1957 by Tested Recipe Institute, Inc., Jim Heimann Collection.

28. Large-letter linen postcard, ca. 1940.

29. *Manatee County Florida*, travel booklet, 1920s.

30. (top) Large-letter linen postcard, 1948; (bottom) illustration from *Big Boy Barbecue Book* ©1956, 1957 by Tested Recipe Institute, Inc., Jim Heimann Collection.

31. (clockwise from top left) *How To Be a Cookout Champion* booklet ©1959 Kaiser Aluminum & Chemical Corp, courtesy of Kaiser Aluminum, Jim Heimann Collection; *Brunswick, St. Simons Island and Sea Island, Georgia,* travel brochure, ca. 1930s; linen postcard, 1947.

32. Large-letter chrome postcard, ca. 1960s.

33. (clockwise from top left) *Hawaii: The Year Round Playground,* travel booklet, 1922; postcard, ca. 1960, Lew Baer Collection; Matson Line menu cover, ca. 1930s.

34. Large-letter linen postcard, 1948.

35. (left) Linen postcard, 1950; (right) *Colorful Sun Valley, Idaho,* travel brochure, ca. 1950s.

36. (top) Large-letter linen postcard, 1951; (bottom) illustration from *Big Boy Barbecue Book* ©1956, 1957 by Tested Recipe Institute, Inc., Jim Heimann Collection.

37. Decatur, Illinois, *The Playground of Central Illinois,* travel brochure, ca. 1920s.

38. Large-letter linen postcard, ca. 1940s.

39. (left) Kwik Chick Sign, San Angelo, TX, photograph ©1982 John Margolies/Esto; (right) *Indiana: The Hoosier State,* travel booklet, ca. 1940.

40. (top) Large-letter linen postcard, ca. 1940s; (bottom) continental chrome postcard, ca. 1980.

41. (left) Linen postcard, ca. 1950; (right) *The Iowa Great Lakes,* travel brochure, ca. 1930.

42. Large-letter linen postcard, ca. 1940.

43. (left) Cohen's Restaurant Sign, Junction City, KS. Photograph ©1980 John Margolies/Esto; (right) *Kansas Travel and Recreation Guide,* travel booklet, 1958.

44. (top) Large-letter linen postcard, ca. 1940; (bottom) illustration from *Big Boy Barbecue Book* ©1956, 1957 by Tested

Recipe Institute, Inc., Jim Heimann Collection.

45. (left) *How to Be a Successful Beginner at Barbecuing* booklet cover, ca. 1950s, Jim Heimann Collection; (right) *Kentucky Parks,* travel brochure, ca. 1960.

46. (top) Large-letter linen postcard, ca. 1940; (bottom) linen postcard, 1949.

47. (left) Christie's Restaurant Sign, Houston, TX, photograph ©1978 John Margolies/Esto; (right) *The New Orleans Visitor's Guide,* ca. 1930s.

48. (top) Large-letter linen postcard, 1942; (bottom) real photo postcard, ca. 1950.

49. (left) Fenton's Seafood Market, Trenton, ME, photograph ©2000 John Margolies/Esto; (right) *Maine Seafood Cookouts,* booklet cover, ca. 1960s, Jim Heimann Collection.

50. Large-letter linen postcard, ca. 1940.

51. (left) *Ocean City, Maryland,* travel brochure, 1948; (right) matchbook cover, ca. 1940s.

52. (top) Large-letter linen postcard, ca. 1940; (bottom) 4 State Poultry Supply, Springdale, AR, photograph ©1984 John Margolies/ Esto.

53. *The Real Tour to the Berkshires,* map booklet cover, ca. 1920s

54. Turkey Roost Restaurant Sign, Bay City, MI, photograph ©1988 John Margolies/Esto.

55. *Visitor's Guide of Boston,* travel brochure, ca. 1950s.

56. Large-letter linen postcard, ca. 1940.

57. (clockwise from top left) Real photo postcard of Legs Inn, Cross Village, MI; *Here's Your Michigan,* 1947; real photo postcard of Pickle Barrel Building, Grand Marais, MI, ca. 1940s.

58. (top) Large-letter linen postcard, 1940; (bottom) Capt. Bobs BBQ Bull, Ocean City, MD, photograph ©1985 John Margolies/Esto.

59. (left) Linen postcard, 1938; (right) *Detroit Lakes, Minnesota,* travel booklet, 1933.

60. Large-letter linen postcard, ca. 1940.

61. (left) Colonel's Catch #2 Sign, High Point, NC, photograph ©1982 John Margolies/Esto; (right) *Gulfport: Where Your Ship Comes In,* travel booklet, ca. 1930s.

62. (top) Large-letter linen postcard, ca. 1940; (bottom) *How to Be a Successful Beginner at Barbecuing* booklet cover illustration, ca. 1950s, Jim Heimann Collection.

63. (left) Phil's Bar-B-Q Sign, St. Louis, MO, photograph ©1988 John Margolies/ Esto; (right) *Missouri's Lake of the Ozarks,* travel brochure, ca. 1940s.

64. (top) Large-letter linen postcard, ca. 1940; (bottom) illustration from *Big Boy Barbecue Book* ©1956, 1957 by Tested Recipe Institute, Inc., Jim Heimann Collection.

65. *Montana Highway Map 1939,* cover.

66. (top) Large-letter linen postcard, ca. 1940; (bottom) linen postcard, ca. 1940s.

67. *Lincoln, Live a Little,* travel brochure, ca. 1970.

68. (top) Large-letter linen postcard, ca. 1940; (bottom) Valley View Lodge Sign, Chittenango, NY, photograph ©1988 John Margolies/Esto.

69. (left) *Las Vegas and Boulder Dam, Nevada,* travel brochure, 1939; (right) *About Nevada,* travel brochure, 1956.

70. (top) Large-letter linen postcard, ca. 1940; (bottom) Black River Falls Oasis Stag Statue, Black River Falls, WI, photograph ©1988 John Margolies/Esto.

71. *New Hampshire Vacation Information,* travel brochure, ca. 1940.

72. (top) Large-letter linen postcard, 1941; (bottom) illustration from *Big Boy Barbecue Book* ©1956, 1957 by Tested Recipe Institute, Inc., Jim Heimann Collection.

73. *Atlantic City; The Playground of the Nation,* travel booklet, 1923.

74. Large-letter linen postcard, ca. 1940.

75. (left) linen postcard, 1935; (right) *Recreational Map of New Mexico, Land of Enchantment,* travel brochure,

76. Large-letter linen postcard, 1952.

77. (left) Linen postcard, ca. 1950; (right) *Empire Tours of New York,* travel booklet, 1926.

78. Large-letter linen postcard, ca. 1940.

79. *Opportunities Agricultural and Industrial,* travel booklet, 1918.

80. (top) Large-letter linen postcard, ca. 1940; (bottom) linen postcard, 1950.

81. (left) Cover of the *Big Boy Barbecue Book* ©1956, 1957 by Tested Recipe Institute, Inc., Jim Heimann Collection; (right) *North Dakota: Where the Sunshine Spends the Winter,* travel brochure, 1957.

82. Large-letter linen postcard, 1937.

83. (left) Linen postcard, ca. 1940s; (right) *Newark and Licking County,* travel brochure, 1936.

84. (top) Large-letter linen postcard; (bottom) Longhorn Café, Amado, AZ, photograph ©1991 John Margolies/Esto.

85. (left) *Grand Lake and Spavinaw Lake of Oklahoma,* travel brochure, ca. 1950; (right) *Better Homes and Gardens Barbeque Book,* ©1956 by Meredith Publishing Company, Jim Heimann Collection.

86. Large-letter linen postcard, ca. 1940.

87. (left) Chrome postcard, ca. 1950s, Sharon Wolf Collection; (right) *Drive Oregon Highways,* travel booklet, 1936.

88. (top) Large-letter linen postcard, ca. 1940; (bottom) illustration from *Big Boy Barbecue Book* ©1956, 1957 by Tested Recipe Institute, Inc., Jim Heimann Collection.

89. (left) Beef Burger Sign, Amarillo, TX, photograph ©1982 John

Margolies/Esto; (right) *This is Pennsylvania,* travel booklet, ca. 1940s.

90. Large-letter linen postcard, 1939.

91. (left) Feature matchbook matches, ca. 1950; (right) *Rhode Island For Relaxation,* travel booklet, 1942.

92. Large-letter linen postcard, ca. 1940.

93. *Myrtle Beach, South Carolina,* travel brochure, ca. 1950s.

94. Large-letter linen postcard, ca. 1940.

95. (clockwise from top left) The Chuck Wagon Café Menu, ca. 1950s; *Visit Sioux Falls,* travel brochure, ca. 1950; chrome postcard, ca. 1960s; chrome postcard, ca. 1970.

96. (top) Large-letter linen postcard; (bottom) Hot Pit Bar-B-Q Sign, photograph ©1979 John Margolies/Esto.

97. (left) *Enjoy Chattanooga,* travel brochure, ca. 1950; (right) chrome postcard, ca. 1950, Lew Baer Collection.

98. (top) Large-letter linen postcard, ca. 1940; (bottom) Big Texan Steak Ranch Bull Statue, Amarillo, TX, photograph ©1982 John Margolies/Esto.

99. *Now That You're Here, See and Know El Paso,* travel brochure, ca. 1950.

100. Large-letter linen postcard, ca. 1940.

101. (left) Linen postcard, ca. 1940s; (right) *The New Saltair and Salt Lake City,* travel brochure, ca. 1910.

102. (clockwise from top) Large-letter linen postcard, ca. 1940; travel decal, ca. 1950, Jim Heimann Collection; illustration from *Big Boy Barbecue Book* ©1956, 1957 by Tested Recipe Institute, Inc., Jim Heimann Collection.

103. (left) 4 States Poultry Supply Chicken Statue, Springdale, AR, photograph ©1984 John Margolies/Esto; (right) *Vermont State Parks and Forests,* travel brochure, ca. 1950s.

104. (top) Large-letter linen postcard,

ca. 1940; (bottom) illustration from *Big Boy Barbecue Book* ©1956, 1957 by Tested Recipe Institute, Inc., Jim Heimann Collection.

105. *All Expense Cruise Tours: Virginia,* travel booklet, 1937.

106. Large-letter linen postcard, ca. 1940.

107. (left) Chrome postcard, ca. 1950s, Lew Baer Collection; (right) *Scenic Guide and Map: Puget Sound Area,* travel brochure, 1955.

108: (top) Large-letter linen postcard, 1937; (bottom) illustration from *Big Boy Barbecue Book* ©1956, 1957 by Tested Recipe Institute, Inc., Jim Heimann Collection.

109. (left) Magazine advertisement detail, courtesy of Leland and Crystal Payton; (right) *West Virginia by Rail and Trail,* travel booklet, 1927.

110. (top) Large-letter linen postcard, ca. 1940; (bottom) illustration from *Big Boy Barbecue Book* ©1956, 1957 by Tested Recipe Institute, Inc., Jim Heimann Collection.

111. *Wisconsin Vacation-Land of Woods and Waters, Where Miles are Smiles,* travel booklet, 1933.

112. Large-letter linen postcard, 1946.

113. (left) *Cheyenne, Wyoming,* travel brochure, ca. 1930s; (right) matchbook cover, ca. 1940.

114. Paper plate, ca. 1960s, Leland and Crystal Payton Collection.

115. Magazine advertisement detail, Saturday Evening Post, ca. 1950s, Jim Heimann Collection.

120. Magazine advertisement, ca 1960, Jim Heimann Collection.

Back Cover: (left) *Maine Seafood Cookouts,* booklet cover, ca. 1960s, Jim Heimann Collection; (right) *Better Homes and Gardens Barbeque Book,* ©1956 by Meredith Publishing Company, Jim Heimann Collection.

INDEX

TABLE OF EQUIVALENTS

The exact equivalents in the following table have been rounded for convenience.

LIQUID/DRY MEASURES

U.S.	METRIC
¼ teaspoon	1.25 milliliters
½ teaspoon	2.5 milliliters
1 teaspoon	5 milliliters
1 tablespoon (3 teaspoons)	15 milliliters
1 fluid ounce (2 tablespoons)	30 milliliters
¼ cup	60 milliliters
⅓ cup	80 milliliters
½ cup	120 milliliters
1 cup	240 milliliters
1 pint (2 cups)	480 milliliters
1 quart (4 cups, 32 ounces)	960 milliliters
1 gallon (4 quarts)	3.84 liters
1 ounce (by weight)	28 grams
1 pound	454 grams
2.2 pounds	1 kilogram

LENGTH

U.S.	METRIC
⅛ inch	3 millimeters
¼ inch	6 millimeters
½ inch	12 millimeters
1 inch	2.5 centimeters

OVEN TEMPERATURE

FAHRENHEIT	CELSIUS	GAS
250	120	½
275	140	1
300	150	2
325	160	3
350	180	4
375	190	5
400	200	6
425	220	7
450	230	8
475	240	9
500	260	10